CAROL VORDERMAN
Spanish Made Easy

10 Minutes A Day

Spanish

Ages
7–11

DK

Authors
Reyes Ávila, Charlotte Tomson
Consultants
Luke Darracott, José Manuel Verdú

10-minute challenge

Try to complete the exercises for each topic in 10 minutes or less. Note the time it takes you in the "Time taken" column below.

Penguin Random House

DK London
Editor Elizabeth Blakemore
Senior Editor Cécile Landau
Managing Editor Christine Stroyan
Managing Art Editor Anna Hall
Spanish Consultants Luke Darracott, José Manuel Verdú
Senior Production Editor Andy Hilliard
Senior Production Controller Jude Crozier
Jacket Design Development Manager Sophia MTT
Publisher Andrew Macintyre
Associate Publishing Director Liz Wheeler
Art Director Karen Self
Publishing Director Jonathan Metcalf

DK Delhi
Senior Editor Rupa Rao
Assistant Editor Kritika Gupta
Art Editor Rashika Kachroo
Project Art Editor Tanvi Nathyal
Managing Editors Soma B. Chowdhury, Kingshuk Ghoshal
Managing Art Editors Ahlawat Gunjan, Govind Mittal
DTP Designers Anita Yadav, Dheeraj Singh, Rakesh Kumar, Harish Aggarwal
Senior Jacket Designer Suhita Dharamjit
Jackets Editorial Coordinator Priyanka Sharma

This edition published in 2020
First published in Great Britain in 2016 by
Dorling Kindersley Limited
DK, One Embassy Gardens, 8 Viaduct Gardens,
London, SW11 7BW

The authorised representative in the EEA is
Dorling Kindersley Verlag GmbH. Arnulfstr. 124,
80636 Munich, Germany

Copyright © 2016, 2020 Dorling Kindersley Limited
A Penguin Random House Company
10 9 8 7
007–285762–May/2020

A CIP catalogue record for this book
is available from the British Library.
ISBN: 978-0-2412-2532-5

Printed and bound in the China

All images © Dorling Kindersley Limited

www.dk.com

MIX
Paper | Supporting responsible forestry
FSC™ C018179

This book was made with Forest Stewardship Council™ certified paper – one small step in DK's commitment to a sustainable future.
Learn more at www.dk.com/uk/information/sustainability

Contents

Time taken

4

¡Hola! ¿Cómo estás?

Practise speaking Spanish by introducing yourself, greeting other people and saying how you are. **¡Vamos!**

(1) **Buenos días** means "good morning" and the more informal **hola** can be translated as "hello" or "hi". Write the best greeting for each of these people.

your friend .... a policeman ....

your teacher .... your mother ....

(2) Here are three Spanish expressions that you might use to say how you feel. Draw lines to match each one to a picture below.

Mal.   Normal.   Bien, gracias.

(3) To be polite, use **señor** (sir), **señora** (madam) and **señorita** (miss) with your greetings. Say **adiós** (goodbye) politely to the people in these pictures.

....

Time filler:
Write down the names of some of your friends. Use the Internet to check if there is a Spanish equivalent of each name. Practise greeting your friends in Spanish, using equivalent Spanish names where possible.

4 Here are two ways of asking "What is your name?" in Spanish, but the vowels are missing. Add the vowels to complete each sentence.

¿C _ m _ t _ ll _ m _ s?

¿C _ _ l _ s t _ n _ mbr _ ?

5 Match each Spanish name with its English equivalent.

Juan   Pedro   María   Carlos   Lucía

Mary   John   Lucy   Peter   Charles

6 Translate each phrase from English to Spanish. Use the Spanish equivalent of people's names.

Goodbye, John!   ....

My name is Mary.   ....

How are you, Lucy?   ....

7 The words in these greetings are all mixed up. Unscramble them and write each sentence correctly.

gracias. Bien, ...

te llamas? ¿Cómo   ....

señora! ¡Buenos días, ...

Los números 1–20

When learning the numbers in any language, it is best to practise them in groups of ten or twenty. Try saying them backwards. Have a go at counting from a random number.

1 A rocket is about to be launched. Below is the countdown in Spanish, but some of the numbers are missing. Fill in the gaps.

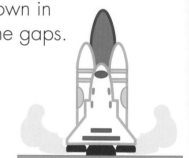

diez, nueve,_____, siete,_____,_____,

cuatro,_____,_____,_____,

cero! Fuego!

2 Write the number for each Spanish number word.

uno	....	dos	....	cuatro	....
siete	....	ocho	....	diez	....
once	....	doce	....	trece	....
quince	....	diecisiete	....	veinte	....

3 Complete each calculation in Spanish.

diez + siete = ...   ocho + dos   = ...

cinco + siete = ...   doce – uno   = ...

tres x dos   = ...   veinte – cinco = ...

4 Circle the even numbers.

uno   cuatro   doce   once   diecisiete

Time filler:
Shuffle a pack of playing cards and then place it face down. Take the top card, turn it over and say the number on it aloud in Spanish. Repeat until you have gone through all the cards. If you pick a Jack, Queen or King, move on to the next card.

5 Translate each number into Spanish. Then complete the crossword.

Across

1. two
2. eleven
3. three
4. twelve
5. nine

Down

1. eight
2. twenty
3. ten
4. seven
5. thirteen

Mi familia

These exercises will give you plenty of practice
at using the words you will need to describe
your family and your friends' families.

1 Read the information given in the chart below. Then use it to
write the name of the child shown in each picture.

Me llamo Alfonso. Tengo una hermana y un hermano.	Me llamo Sofía. Tengo dos hermanos.
Me llamo Elena. Tengo una hermana. No tengo un hermano.	Me llamo José. No tengo ni hermanos ni hermanas.

....

....

....

....

2 Translate these phrases. Remember to use the correct Spanish word
for "my" (**mi** or **mis**) in each case.

my brothers .... my mother ....

my grandmother .... my sisters ....

Time filler:
Write a brief description of everyone in your family or of each of your friends, in Spanish. Use a dictionary to help you.

3 Look at the people in this family. Then complete each sentence.

El padre se llama… .... La madre se llama… ....

El abuelo se llama… .... La abuela se llama… ....

El niño pequeño se llama… .... La hermana se llama… ....

Los bebés se llaman… ....

Los niños se llaman… ....

4 Circle the correct form of the verb **llamarse** (to be called) in each sentence.

Mis hermanos se llama / se llaman Adrián y Carlos.

La hermana de David se llama / se llaman Elena.

Mis padres se llama / se llaman Lucas y María.

¿Cuántos años tienes?

In Spanish, we use the verb **tener** (to have) to say how old we are. For example, to say that you are nine years old in Spanish, you would say, **"Tengo nueve años."**

1. Look at each picture. Then complete each sentence by writing the missing word.

Tengo _____ años.

Tengo _____ años.

Tengo _____ años.

Tengo _____ años.

Tengo _____ años.

Time filler:
Write down the ages of friends and members of your family. Then practise saying in Spanish how old each one of them is. You could also write down the Spanish sentences you use, if you have time.

2) Here is a sheet from a notebook, showing the names and ages of some children taken on a school trip. Next to it, write sentences in Spanish, stating each child's age. The first one has been done for you.

Nombre	Edad
Pedro	7
Eduardo	11
Miguel	9
Elena	8
Lucas	10
Cristina	12

Pedro tiene siete años.

3) Fill in the missing letters to complete each sentence.

Mi herm__na tiene q__ince a__os.   Ten__o si__te año__.

M__ herm__no ti__ne n__eve año__.   Tengo o__e __ños.

4) Translate these sentences into Spanish.

He is ten.

She is eight years old.

He is fourteen.

She is three.

En mi mochila

In Spanish, all nouns are either masculine or feminine. Also, the Spanish words for "a/an" (**un** and **una**) and "the" (**el** or **la**) vary depending on whether the noun following them is masculine or feminine.

1 Fill in the chart. Add the Spanish word for each object listed in English, as well as the correct Spanish word for "the" (**el** or **la**) that you would use in each case. **Note:** You may use a dictionary to help you.

English	el or la	Spanish
pencil		
pen		
rubber		
pencil case		
calculator		
felt-tip pen		
pencil sharpener		
school bag		
notebook		
ruler		

2 Circle the correct Spanish word for "a/an" in each phrase.

un / una bolsa   un / una regla

un / una goma   un / una lápiz

un / una bolígrafo   un / una estuche

un / una rotulador   un / una calculadora

un / una cuaderno   un / una sacapuntas

Time filler
Empty out your school bag. Write a
description of the contents, using
a dictionary to look up any new word.
Start by writing: **En mi mochila,
tengo...** (In my school bag, I have...).

3) The following sentence is written as a code.

7 1   18 14   18 15 26 3 14 2 4   9 7 1 11 15
25 1 4   6 7 11 2 4.

Use this code-breaking chart to reveal what letter each number in
the coded sentence stands for. Then write the decoded message.

a	b	c	e	g	h	i	l	m	n	o	r	s	t	u	y
4	17	26	7	11	3	14	2	18	1	15	6	23	9	25	13

4) Find the Spanish words for ten classroom objects in this word-search
puzzle. **Hint:** All the words can be found on the chart on page 12.

c	a	l	c	u	l	a	d	o	r	a	è	s
t	a	i	l	l	r	e	g	l	a	b	g	a
y	z	f	c	m	o	h	o	i	c	o	l	c
l	e	r	x	n	t	i	m	t	u	l	e	a
o	b	q	z	s	u	c	a	w	a	í	n	p
m	o	c	h	i	l	a	g	s	d	g	t	u
r	o	t	u	l	a	d	o	r	e	r	o	n
l	á	p	i	z	d	l	a	r	r	a	o	t
b	u	f	p	a	o	i	g	z	n	f	a	a
e	s	t	u	c	h	e	e	t	o	o	b	s

Los números 20–69

Remember that numbers over thirty in Spanish combine the tens and units with a **y** (instead of the dash in English numbers) to make pronunciation easier. For example, **treinta y uno** (thirty-one) and **cuarenta y siete** (forty-seven).

(1) Complete each number word in the chart.

Number	Number word
23	veinti ....
34	.... y cuatro
41	cuarenta y ....
52	.... y dos
69	sesenta y ....

(2) Write these numbers as digits.

treinta y uno ☐   sesenta y siete ☐   veinticuatro ☐

veintiséis ☐   cincuenta y ocho ☐   cuarenta y nueve ☐

(3) Write the Spanish for each number.

51 ....   42 ....   63 ....

29 ....   35 ....   57 ....

(4) Write the next two numbers in each sequence.

veintiuno, veintidós... ....

cuarenta y seis, cuarenta y siete.... ....

Time filler:
Look around your home. Look in books and magazines, at pictures and clocks. Write down any number you see between 20 and 69. Then write the Spanish word for each of these numbers.

5 Solve these sums. Write the answers, first in digits and then in Spanish.

3 x 7 = ☐ ....   6 x 7 = ☐ ....

9 x 3 = ☐ ....   12 x 3 = ☐ ....

6 x 8 = ☐ ....   10 x 5 = ☐ ....

8 x 8 = ☐ ....   11 x 5 = ☐ ....

7 x 9 = ☐ ....   11 x 3 = ☐ ....

6 In this word-search puzzle, find the Spanish words for the ten numbers that are answers to the sums in question 5.

c	u	a	r	e	n	t	a	y	d	o	s	n	q	f	v
i	s	e	s	e	n	t	a	y	c	u	a	t	r	o	e
n	r	t	u	i	p	w	r	p	f	y	q	u	t	v	i
c	t	y	u	p	v	i	n	g	t	-	s	e	p	e	n
u	s	e	s	e	n	t	a	y	t	r	e	s	x	i	t
e	o	i	x	a	n	t	e	-	q	u	a	t	r	n	i
n	u	v	i	n	g	t	-	e	t	-	u	n	e	t	s
t	r	e	i	n	t	a	y	s	e	i	s	t	r	i	i
a	m	i	e	g	h	c	i	n	q	u	a	n	t	u	e
t	r	e	i	n	t	a	y	t	r	e	s	h	u	n	t
c	u	a	r	e	n	t	a	y	o	c	h	o	s	o	e
q	c	i	n	c	u	e	n	t	a	y	c	i	n	c	o

Los meses del año

Unlike in English, the names of the months in Spanish begin with a lower-case letter, for example, **junio** (June).

1 Select Spanish words for the months of the year from the chart below to match the list of months in English.

agosto	enero	septiembre	marzo	noviembre	abril
febrero	mayo	junio	octubre	diciembre	julio

January .... July ....

February .... August ....

March .... September ....

April .... October ....

May .... November ....

June .... December ....

2 Use the first letter and the number of spaces provided as clues to work out the birthday month of each child.

Mi cumpleaños es el 26 de e....... ....

Mi cumpleaños es el 17 de a ....

Mi cumpleaños es el 10 de f....... ....

Mi cumpleaños es el 31 de m....... ....

Time filler:
Make your own Spanish calendar. Divide a large sheet of paper into twelve equal sections and label each section with the name of a month in Spanish. Record important dates and events on your calendar in Spanish, too!

(3) ¿Cuándo es tu cumpleaños?
When is your birthday?

....

(4) The letters have fallen out of the bottom of this puzzle grid! On the way down, they got mixed up, although they are still in their correct rows. Unscramble them to discover the mystery birthday date.

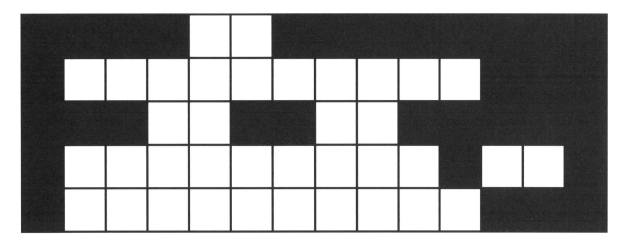

i m

m u l c ñ s a o e p

s e e l

n i t e n i o v u e d

m e e t b p r s e i

(5) Continue this sequence.

marzo   abril   mayo   ....

18

Los adjetivos

In Spanish, adjectives must be in their masculine form when they are used to describe a masculine noun and in their feminine form when used to describe a feminine noun.

1 Write the feminine form and the English translation for each adjective listed on the chart. **Note:** You may use a dictionary to help you.

Spanish (Masculine)	Spanish (Feminine)	English
bueno		
tímido		
glotón		
pequeño		
grande		
deportista		
malo		
bonito		
perezoso		
amable		
divertido		
simpático		

2 Complete the following sentences using adjectives from the chart above.

Soy .... y ....

Mi madre es .... y ....

Time filler:
Practise your Spanish by describing your family or friends. What do they look like? What are their main characteristics? Remember to make the adjectives you use agree with the gender of the person you are describing.

3 Choose your favourite character from a book or a film. Write a few sentences describing him or her in Spanish.

....

....

....

....

4 Circle the adjective in each Spanish sentence that correctly matches the English sentences.

He has brown hair.	Él tiene el pelo marrón / rojo / rubio / negro.
She has red hair.	Ella tiene el pelo marrón / rojo / rubio / negro.
He has green eyes.	Él tiene los ojos marrones / azules / verdes / grises.
She has blue eyes.	Ella tiene los ojos marrones / azules / verdes / grises.

5 Write a brief description of yourself in Spanish. Use **Soy**… (I am…) and **Tengo**… (I have…) to begin your sentences.

....

....

....

....

Beat the clock 1

Write the correct present tense form
of the verbs shown in brackets below.
Remember that they are all regular verbs,
ending in **-er**. How many can you do in
10 minutes? **¡Vamos!**

Yo (comer) ....

Él (comer) ....

Ella (prometer) ....

Yo (romper) ....

Tú (romper) ....

Nosotros (romper) ....

Él (comprender) ....

Él (romper) ....

Él (prometer) ....

Tú (prometer) ....

Tú (comer) ....

Ella (aprender) ....

Nosotros (comer) ....

Ellos (comer) ....

Vosotros (correr) ....

Ella (comer) ....

Ellos (romper) ....

Él (aprender) ....

Ellos (prometer) ....

Vosotros (romper) ....

Ellas (romper) ....

Él (responder) ....

Él (correr) ....

Ellas (aprender) ....

Yo (correr) ....

Yo (vender) ....

Tú (aprender) ....

Tú (comprender) ....

Time filler:
Translate each infinitive verb in the list below into English. Keep testing yourself on these verbs – their meaning and present tense. They are used frequently in Spanish and you will need to be familiar with them.

Ella (meter) ....

Vosotros (comer) ....

Yo (responder) ....

Tú (responder) ....

Él (vender) ....

Él (meter) ....

Tú (meter) ....

Tú (depender) ....

Ella (romper) ....

Tú (vender) ....

Ellas (prometer) ....

Ellas (comer) ....

Él (depender) ....

Yo (meter) ....

Ellas (comprender) ....

Ella (responder) ....

Ellos (aprender) ....

Vosotros (prometer) ....

Nosotros (aprender) ....

Vosotros (comprender) ....

Vosotros (apender) ....

Nosotros (meter) ....

Nosotros (comprender) ....

Ellos (comprender) ....

Ella (comprender) ....

Vosotros (depender) ....

Nosotros (prometer) ....

Nosotros (depender) ....

Los colores

Spanish words for colours must be written in their masculine, feminine or plural form, depending on the gender of the noun they are describing and whether it is singular or plural.

1 Translate the English colour words into Spanish.

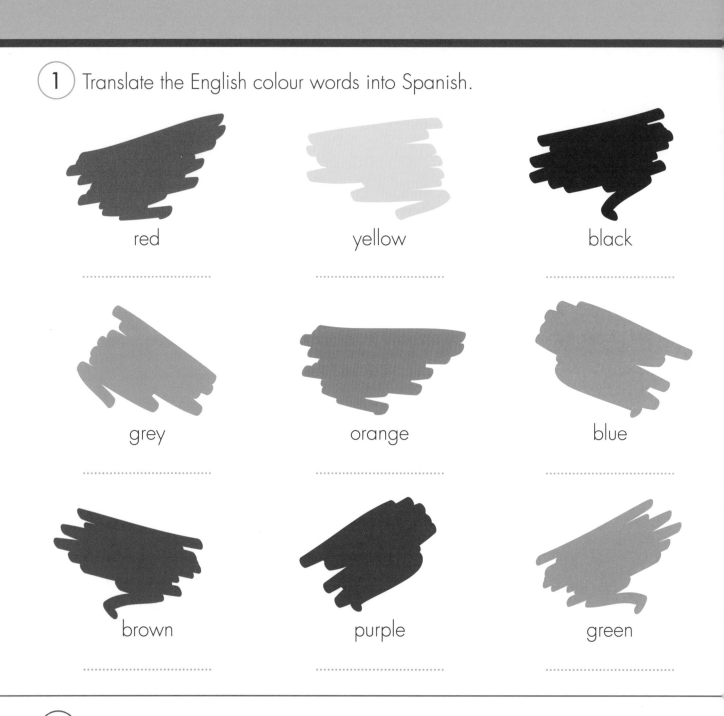

red

yellow

black

grey

orange

blue

brown

purple

green

2 Unscramble these Spanish colour words.

anbclo ....

joor ....

jaanarn ....

rómran ....

erdev ....

rallimao ....

Time filler:
Look up the Spanish for shades of
the same basic colours in a dictionary.
For example, **azul marino** (navy blue)
and **azul turquesa** (turquoise blue)
are shades of the same colour. How
many can you find?

3 Fill in the chart by writing the different Spanish forms of each colour given in English.

English	Spanish (Masculine/Plural)	Spanish (Feminine/Plural)
red		
yellow		
blue		
green		
brown		
orange		
white		
black		
grey		
purple		
pink		

4 Spot the mistakes! Write each phrase using the correct form of the adjective.

una goma morado ....

unos lápices marrón ....

un sombrero roja ....

mi vestido blancos ....

Los días de la semana

Remember that days (and months) in Spanish start with a lower-case letter – unlike in English, where they have an initial capital letter.

1 Draw a line linking each day in Spanish to its English equivalent.

martes	Sunday
sábado	Monday
jueves	Tuesday
lunes	Wednesday
miércoles	Thursday
domingo	Friday
viernes	Saturday

2 Continue each sequence.

martes ....

viernes ....

domingo ....

miércoles ....

Time filler:
Make two sets of seven cards. On one set, write the days of the week in Spanish, a day on each card. On the other set, do the same, but write the days in English. Shuffle together both sets of cards. Then arrange the cards face up. How quickly you can match the English and Spanish words?

(3) Complete these sentences.

Antes del martes, es ....

Después del sábado, es ....

Antes del viernes, es ....

Después del lunes, es ....

lunes

martes

miércoles

jueves

viernes

sábado

domingo

(4) Translate the following dates into Spanish.

Monday, 3rd July ....

Saturday, 1st September ....

Wednesday, 5th January ....

(5) Answer the questions in Spanish.

What is the date tomorrow? ....

What was the date yesterday? ....

What will the date be
in two days' time? ....

Los animales

Talking about animals is a good way to practise expressing yourself in Spanish. What is your favourite animal?

1 In each pair, circle the smaller animal. Use a dictionary to look up any word that you do not know.

un perro	un elefante
un gato	un tigre
un caballo	un ratón
un pájaro	un gorila
un conejo	una abeja
una rana	una oveja

2 Unscramble the sentences below.

perros. tiene dos Pedro   ....

Sofía tres tiene caballos.   ....

tiene cuatro David pájaros.   ....

3 Which animals do you prefer? Answer in full sentences.

¿Tú prefieres los gatos o los perros?

....

¿Tú prefieres las tortugas o los peces dorados?

....

Time filler:
Create a poster for your ideal zoo or
tienda de animales (pet shop).
Label the animals in Spanish. Write a
short paragraph describing how many
there are of each kind of animal.
Start with **Hay...** (There are...).

4 Work out which animal is making the sounds.

miau

¿Cuál es el animal que hace miau?

....

cuac cuac

¿Cuál es el animal que hace cuac cuac?

....

kikiriki

¿Cuál es el animal que hace kikiriki?

....

¿Cuál es el animal que hace guau guau?

....

guau guau

5 Read out the list of animals in the box below.

| la rana | la vaca | la oveja | el tigre | el pato | el gorila |

Now sort the animals by where you are most likely to see each one.

¿en el lago?   ¿en la granja?   ¿en el zoo?

....

....

La casa

Help yourself learn the Spanish words for the various rooms in your house by placing flash cards showing the words on walls and doors.

① Translate these words into English. **Note:** You may use a dictionary to help you.

el salón	....	el despacho	....
el ático	....	el sótano	....
la cocina	....	el baño	....
la habitación	....	el comedor	....
las escaleras	....	el jardín	....
la bodega	....	la habitación infantil	....

② Look at these lists of things you might find in some of the rooms in your house. Circle the object in each list that would be out of place.

La cocina:
el fregadero
la almohada
el frigo
el horno

El salón:
el fregadero
el sofá
las cortinas
el sillón

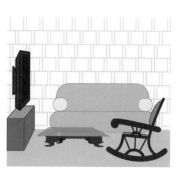

La habitación:
la cama
la alfombra
la almohada
el horno

El baño:
la ducha
el lavabo
la cama
la toalla

Time filler:
Write a description of your house. Start your sentences with **En el sótano, hay...** (In the basement, there is...), **En la planta baja, hay...** (On the ground floor, there is...), **En la primera planta, hay...** (On the first floor, there is...), and so on.

3 Look at the picture. Then answer the questions below in Spanish.

¿Qué hay en la planta baja?

....

....

¿Qué hay en la primera planta?

....

....

¿Qué hay en la segunda planta?

....

....

¿Dónde vives?

What sort of house do you live in? What
is the name of your town or village?
What type of location do you live in?

1 Complete the chart by adding the English translations.

Spanish	English
una casa	
un piso	
una casa pareada	
un chalet	
una casa adosada	
un bungalow	

2 Find out what the Spanish expressions mean by unscrambling
their English translations.

Spanish	English		
en la ciudad	in tnow	=	
en el campo	in the cidentrouys	=	
en las afueras	in the rbssubu	=	
en las montañas	in the itmounasn	=	
en la playa/junto al mar	by the esa	=	

Time filler:
Think of a character from one of your favourite storybooks. Try to describe in Spanish where he or she lives and in what type of house. Is it in the country or in a town? Is it in the mountains or in the woods? Is it near a river or lake, or by the sea?

3 Insert the correct form of the present tense of the verb **vivir** (to live) in these sentences.

Yo .... en Londres.

Él .... en la playa.

Tú .... en las afueras.

Ellos .... en el campo.

Nosotros .... en la ciudad.

Vosotros .... en un pueblo.

4 Translate these Spanish sentences into English.

Vivo con mis padres en una casa adosada.

....

Ella vive con su madre en un piso grande.

....

5 Translate these English sentences into Spanish.

My grandparents live on an old farm in the mountains.

....

My cousins live in a bungalow by the sea.

....

Los países

Remember that "in" translates as **en** and "to" translates as **a** in Spanish before the name of a country or city, regardless of whether the country or city name is masculine or feminine.

1 Translate these sentences from English to Spanish.
Note: You may use a dictionary to help you.

I live in France.

....

I live by the sea in Greece.

....

I work in the Netherlands.

....

He lives in the mountains in Italy.

....

She lives in Canada.

....

He is going to Wales.

....

I am going to the USA.

....

She lives in Spain.

....

They live in the countryside in Portugal.

....

Time filler:
Look up the Spanish words for various nationalities in a dictionary. Then write the nationalities and the country names associated with them in pairs. Use a capital letter for the country and a lower case letter for the nationality, for example, **Inglaterra, inglés.**

2 Fill in the chart by writing the Spanish name for each country.
Note: You may use a dictionary to help you.

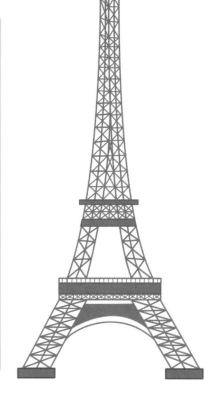

English	Spanish
Scotland	
England	
Ireland	
Belgium	
Germany	
Denmark	
Switzerland	
Turkey	
Norway	

3 Translate the sentences below from English to Spanish.

I work in London. ....

I am going to Barcelona. ....

I live in Paris. ....

4 Write the correct Spanish word for "in" or "to" that you would use in these sentences.

Yo vivo .... Nueva York.   Yo voy .... California.

En la ciudad

These exercises will help you learn the Spanish for places around town that you might want to visit, such as shops, museums and restaurants. Pay special attention to the gender of nouns.

1 Complete the chart by adding the English translations.
Note: You may use a dictionary to help you.

Spanish	English
el supermercado	
la oficina de correos	
la escuela	
el banco	
el parque	
el museo	
la biblioteca	
el café	
el hospital	
la estación	
la piscina	
el restaurante	

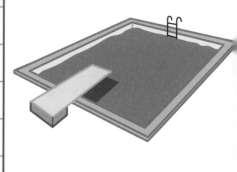

2 Answer these questions in Spanish.

¿Dónde se compra la carne? ....

¿Dónde se compran las tartas? ....

¿Dónde se compra el pan? ....

Time filler:
Describe your town. Start with the phrase, **En mi ciudad, hay...** (In my town, there is/are...). You could also practise saying what your town lacks, using the phrase **No hay...** (There is/are no...).

3) Complete this chart by adding the correct form of the present tense of the verb **ir** (to go).

English	Spanish
I go	Yo ....
You (singular) go	Tú ....
He/she goes	Él/Ella ....
We go	Nosotros ....
You (plural) go	Vosotros ....
They go	Ellos/Ellas ....

4) Choose the right way to say "to" – **al** or **a la** – to complete the phrases below.

Yo voy .... hotel.

Tú vas .... colegio.

Ellos van .... piscina.

Nosotros vamos .... estación de servicio.

5) Use the right form of the verb **ir** (to go) and the right way of saying "to" to complete the sentences below.

Sofía .... iglesia.

Nosotros .... tiendas.

Él .... hospital.

Ellos .... estadio.

Yo .... restaurante.

¿Tú .... banco?

Ellas .... peluquería.

Mis padres .... museos.

¿Dónde está…?

Practise asking people for directions in Spanish and listen carefully to the answer to make sure you understand it! Can you describe the location and position of buildings in Spanish?

(1) Unscramble these sentences to reveal three requests for directions.

¿Cómo llegar puedo a estación? la

....

Disculpe señora, ir oficina de correos? a la¿ para

....

Disculpe señor, el ¿ dónde está restaurante?

....

(2) Draw lines linking the Spanish phrases with their English translations.

enfrente de	between
cerca de	opposite
entre	near
al lado de	in front of
delante de	behind
detrás de	next to

(3) Choose from **del, de la, de los** or **de las** to complete the directions below.

Hay una oficina de correos enfrente .... estación.

Hay un banco cerca .... hotel.

Hay una oficina de turismo cerca .... tiendas.

Time filler:
Draw a map of your neighbourhood or local town centre. Label some of the places and buildings in Spanish. Put a dot and write **Tu estás aquí** (You are here) next to it. Write directions in Spanish from this position to different places on the map.

(4) Translate these English sentences into Spanish.

The bank is between the church and the museum.

....

My school is near my house and the park.

....

The library is next to the café and the station.

....

(5) Look at these symbols for various directions.

Siga todo recto

Gire a la derecha

Gire a la izquierda

Coja la segunda calle a la derecha

Coja la primera calle a la izquierda

Now write in Spanish what the sequences of symbols below mean:

....

....

....

El tiempo libre

Remember that you use the verb **hacer** or **practicar** when you want to say that you "do" any activity, but you use **jugar al/a la** when you want to say that you "play" a sport.

1 Fill in the chart by ticking (✔) the correct column to say which of the sports listed is masculine or feminine, and adding the English translation.
Note: You may use a dictionary to help you.

Spanish	Masculine	Feminine	English
tenis			
fútbol			
equitación			
natación			
gimnasia			
esquí			
windsurf			

2 Use the correct form of the verb **practicar** (to practise) to complete the sentences below.

Yo _____ el esquí.

Nosotros _____ la equitación.

Tú _____ la natación.

Él _____ la gimnasia.

Time filler:
Design a timetable for your own leisure centre.
Label each column with a day of the week:
lunes, martes, miércoles and so on.
Under each day, list the sports and other
activities on offer.

3 Write the correct form of **jugar al/a la** or **practicar** to complete
each sentence.

Ellas .... el patinaje.   Yo .... la natación.

Tú .... tenis.   Él .... la gimnasia.

Nosotros .... fútbol.   Vosotros .... rugby.

4 Write about which sports you like and which you dislike by completing
the following sentences.

Me gusta ....

No me gusta ....

Me encanta ....

Yo odio ....

Mi deporte favorito es ....

5 Choose the correct verb from the box below to complete the sentences.

| escuchar   ir   montar   leer |

Me gusta .... en bici.

Me gusta .... los libros.

Me gusta .... a las tiendas.

Me gusta .... la música.

¿Qué hora es?

Practise telling the time in Spanish.
Remember that **hora** is a feminine
noun, so "one o'clock" will be **la una**
in Spanish and "half past one" will be
la una y media.

① Draw lines to match the time on each clock with the correct sentence.

Son las seis.   Son las nueve.   Son las tres.

② Add **y cuarto, y media** or **menos cuarto** to complete the Spanish
translations on the chart below.

English	Spanish
It is quarter past two.	Son las dos ....
It is quarter past one.	Es la una ....
It is half past five.	Son las cinco ....
It is half past four.	Son las cuatro ....
It is quarter to ten.	Son las diez ....
It is quarter to eleven.	Son las once ....

③ Unscramble these English sentences. Then translate them into Spanish.

I'ts madyid.   ....

Its' nhtigmdi.   ....

Time filler:
Use simple drawings to show your morning routine – getting up, washing and dressing, having breakfast and brushing your teeth. Under the picture of each activity, write the time that you usually do it in Spanish.

4 Circle the correct sentence to match the time on each clock.

Son las dos.   Son las cuatro menos cuarto.

Es la una y diez.   Son las dos menos cuarto.

Son las cinco.   Son las tres menos cuarto.

5 Write the time shown on the digital clocks in Spanish.

 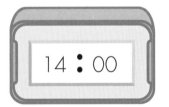 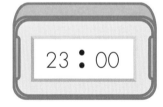

6 Answer these questions about how you spend your evening. To say at a specific time, use **a** + the time, for example, **a las ocho** (at eight o'clock).

¿A qué hora haces tus deberes?

¿A qué hora ves la televisión?

Beat the clock 2

Write the correct present tense form of the verbs shown in brackets below. Remember that they are all regular verbs that end in **-ir**. **¡Vamos!**

Yo (vivir) ....

Tú (existir) ....

Él (insistir) ....

Nosotros (vivir) ....

Ellos (existir) ....

Ella (permitir) ....

Yo (decidir) ....

Nosotros (decidir) ....

Yo (subir) ....

Él (compartir) ....

Tú (sufrir) ....

Ella (existir) ....

Nosotros (recibir) ....

Ellas (permitir) ....

Ella (insistir) ....

Él (permitir) ....

Tú (vivir) ....

Yo (existir) ....

Ellos (insistir) ....

Ellos (permitir) ....

Tú (decidir) ....

Vosotros (vivir) ....

Tú (subir) ....

Él (sufrir) ....

Tú (recibir) ....

Yo (compartir) ....

Vosotros (decidir) ....

Yo (insistir) ....

Time filler:
Translate each infinitive verb in the list below into English. Keep testing yourself on these verbs – their meaning and present tense. They are used frequently in Spanish and you will need to be familiar with them.

Él (vivir) ....

Nosotros (existir) ....

Tú (insistir) ....

Vosotros (permitir) ....

Él (decidir) ....

Él (subir) ....

Ella (sufrir) ....

Ellas (vivir) ....

Nosotros (permitir) ....

Tú (compartir) ....

Él (recibir) ....

Ellos (decidir) ....

Ellos (existir) ....

Nosotros (insistir) ....

Yo (permitir) ....

Él (existir) ....

Ella (decidir) ....

Ella (vivir) ....

Vosotros (insistir) ....

Ellas (decidir) ....

Tú (permitir) ....

Ellos (vivir) ....

Vosotros (existir) ....

Ella (subir) ....

Nosotros (sufrir) ....

Él (compartir) ....

Vosotros (recibir) ....

Ellas (insistir) ....

Mi rutina

When you talk about your daily routine in Spanish, you will use reflexive verbs that describe actions you do to yourself, such as **despertarse** (to wake up). You may also use adverbs and time-connective words, such as **luego** (then) and **después** (after), to say in what order things happen.

(1) Choose reflexive pronouns from the box below to complete the different forms of the present tense of the verb **levantarse** (to get up).

se	me	te	os	nos

Yo .... levanto.   Nosotros .... levantamos.

Tú .... levantas.   Vosotros .... levantáis.

Él/Ella .... levanta.   Ellos/Ellas .... levantan.

(2) Draw lines to match the Spanish sentences about your daily routine to their English translation.

Yo me levanto.	I wake up.
Yo me despierto.	I get dressed.
Yo me peino.	I get up.
Yo me ducho.	I comb my hair.
Yo me acuesto.	I brush my teeth.
Yo me visto.	I have a shower.
Yo me lavo los dientes.	I go to bed.
Yo como/almuerzo.	I read a book.
Yo leo un libro.	I have lunch.

Time filler:
Make a word snake! Ask a friend to write a list in Spanish of what he or she does each morning, but with no spaces between the words. Can you put the spaces in the right places and work out his or her routine?

(3) Write the English for these Spanish adverbs. **Note:** You may use a dictionary to help you.

normalmente

....

a menudo

....

de vez en cuando

....

raramente

....

(4) Complete the following sentences by adding an adverb to say how often you do the after-school activities mentioned.

Yo leo ....

Yo salgo con mis amigos ....

Yo veo la televisión ....

Yo hago mis deberes ....

Yo escucho la música ....

(5) Read the paragraph in Spanish below. Underline the time-connective words and phrases.

En primer lugar, yo me despierto. Habitualmente me levanto cinco minutos más tarde. Luego, me lavo, me visto y tomo mi desayuno. Después, me lavo los dientes. Finalmente, me peino.

La ropa

Watch out here for words such as **vaqueros** (jeans),
pantalones (trousers) and **pantalones cortos**
(shorts), which are plural – just as they are in English!

1 Fill the gaps on the chart below. Use a dictionary to look up new words.

Spanish	English
unos pantalones	
unos vaqueros	
	a T-shirt
una blusa	
un abrigo	
un gorro	
	pyjamas
unos pantalones cortos	

Spanish	English
una camisa	
	a dress
	a skirt
una bufanda	
unos guantes	
unos calcetínes	
unos zapatos	
unas sandalias	

2 Discover what people are wearing by using the code-breaking key
to decipher the sentences below.

e = ♠   u = ♥   o = ♣   a = ♦   s = ☼

N♥ri♦ ll♠v♦ ♥n v♠☼tid♣ y ♥n♦☼ ☼♦nd♦li♦☼.

....

♠l♠n♦ ll♠v♦ ♥n♦ f♦ld♦ y ♥n♦ bl♥☼♦.

....

T♣m ll♠v♦ ♥n♣☼ p♦nt♦l♣n♠☼ c♣rt♣☼ y ♥n♦ c♦mi☼♦t♦.

....

Time filler:
Draw a picture of your favourite outfit. Label the items of clothing in Spanish. Add in details about colours and patterns to extend your list. If you have time, draw outfits for different occasions, such as a birthday party, a day at the beach, and so on.

3) In each box, draw a picture of the garment described in Spanish.

una bufanda roja de lunares	un vestido rosa a cuadros	una camiseta blanca a rayas verdes	una falda azul de flores

4) Finish these sentences. Note the use of the past tense (**Yo llevé**/I wore) and the near future tense (**Voy a llevar**/I am going to wear).

Hoy, yo llevo ....

Ayer, yo llevé ....

Mañana, voy a llevar ....

5) Complete these sentences by describing what outfit you will wear.

Para ir al pueblo, yo voy a llevar ....

Para ir a la playa, yo voy a llevar ....

¿Qué tiempo hace?

Remember that when talking about the weather in Spanish, you often use the verb **hacer** (to make). For example, **hace buen tiempo** means "the weather is good" and **hace frío** means "it is cold".

1) Fill in the missing letters in the Spanish descriptions of the weather symbols. **Note:** You may use a dictionary to help you.

Está llov _ _ _ _ _.

Es _ _ nubl _ _ _ _.

Está nev _ _ _ _.

Ha _ tor _ _ _ _ ta.

H _ _ e c _ _ or.

Ha _ _ v _ _ _ to.

Ha _ _ _ f _ _ _ _.

_ _ _ ce s _ _ _.

2) Describe the weather during the different seasons of the year by filling in the gaps in these sentences. The first one has been done for you.

En invierno, _____ nieva _____ y _____ hace frío _____ .

En primavera, _____ y _____ .

En verano, _____ y _____ .

En otoño, _____ y _____ .

3 Complete these sentences, writing what you would wear for the weather described.

Cuando hace calor, yo llevo ....

Cuando hace frío, yo llevo ....

Cuando llueve, yo llevo ....

4 Look at the weather symbols on the map. Then complete the sentences given below the map. The first one has been done for you.

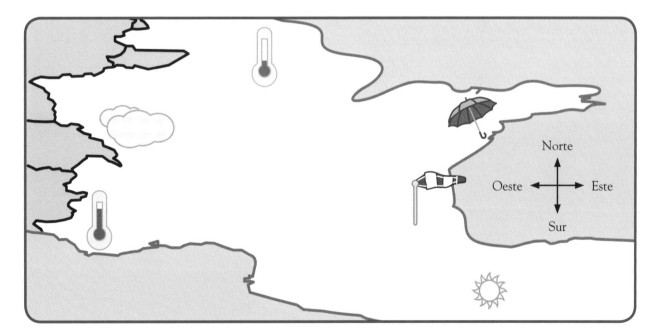

En el norte, ... hace frío ....

En el noreste, ...

En el oeste, ...

En el este, ...

En el sur, ...

En el suroeste, ...

En la escuela

What do you think of the subjects taught in your school? Which ones do you like best? Which ones do you dislike or find difficult? Practise explaining why you think what you think using **porque**... (because...).

1 Fill in the gaps on the chart below, showing some of the subjects taught in school. **Note:** You may use a dictionary to help you.

Spanish	English
	maths
	drama
	science
	Spanish
el dibujo	
el deporte	

Spanish	English
la religión	
la tecnología	
	history
	geography
	music
la informática	

2 Translate these English sentences into Spanish.

Sports is okay, but I hate maths.

....

I also like geography, because it's interesting.

....

Drawing is my favourite subject and sport is great, too!

....

I like history, but drama is awful!

....

Time filler:
Create a timetable for your ideal week at school.
Which subjects would you study? Which ones
would you skip? Remember to use the Spanish
words for days of the week on your timetable.

(3) Say which school subjects you like and which you dislike by filling
in the gaps in these sentences. **Note:** In Spanish, any subject you
mention must always have **el, la** or **las** in front of it.

Me gusta .... porque es ....

No me gusta .... porque es ....

Me gusta mucho .... porque es ....

Yo odio .... porque es ....

(4) Translate these Spanish expressions into English.

¡Es estupendo!   ....

Es interesante.   ....

Es divertido.   ....

¡Es genial!   ....

Es fácil.   ....

Está bien.   ....

Es aburrido.   ....

No es bueno.   ....

Es difícil.   ....

La música

Do you play a musical instrument? Or do you like to sing? Get ready to talk about music on these pages.

1 Add the Spanish translations of the English words to this chart, saying whether they are masculine or feminine nouns.

English	Spanish	Masculine or Feminine
clarinet		
saxophone		
piano		
guitar		
trumpet		
drums		
violin		
cello		

2 Translate these sentences into English.

Me gusta la música clásica.

....

Me gusta mucho la música pop.

....

¡Me encanta la música folclórica!

....

Me gusta también la música de ballet.

....

¡No me gusta la música rock!

....

Time filler:
Find a picture of an orchestra in a magazine or book, or on the Internet. Can you name all of the instruments in Spanish? Use the chart you have filled in on page 52 and a dictionary to help you.

3 Translate these sentences into Spanish. **Note:** To say that you play a musical instrument, you use the verb **tocar** (to touch) + the name of the instrument. The first one has been done for you.

I play the saxophone.   Yo toco el saxofón.

She plays the clarinet.   ....

Do you play the piano?   ....

He plays the violin.   ....

We play the trumpet.   ....

They play the drums.   ....

They play the guitar.   ....

4 Translate what these people are saying into English.

Yo no toco un instrumento, pero me gustan los conciertos.

....

Yo no toco un instrumento, pero me encanta cantar.

....

Yo toco el violín en una orquesta y yo canto en un coro también.

....

Los números 70–1000

Remember that Spanish numbers over seventy continue to combine the tens and units with a **y** (instead of the dash in English numbers) to make pronunciation easier. For example, **setenta y uno** (seventy-one) and **noventa y dos** (ninety-two).

1 Write the Spanish for these numbers.

70 ....

80 ....

90 ....

2 Write the Spanish for these numbers.

200 ....   900 ....

300 ....   700 ....

500 ....   800 ....

3 Reorder the numbers given below, starting with the smallest at the top.

veintiocho   ....

sesenta y tres   ....

noventa y siete   ....

setenta y tres   ....

mil   ....

ochenta y seis   ....

treinta y dos   ....

cuarenta y uno   ....

cien   ....

Time filler:
Find the website of a Spanish department store on the Internet. Look at the prices given in euros. Then try saying and writing out those prices in Spanish.

(4) Draw lines to match the numbers on the left with the number words on the right.

190   ciento treinta y cuatro

172   ciento ochenta y tres

165   ciento noventa

183   ciento setenta y dos

134   ciento sesenta y cinco

(5) Solve these sums. Give your answers first in digits and then in Spanish.

treinta y uno + cuarenta   = ...

treinta + cincuenta y dos   = ...

noventa + once   = ...

(6) Write the Spanish for each amount of money.

€ 30.80   ....

€ 200.78   ....

€ 86.43   ....   €100

€ 282.17   ....   €100

€ 120.00   ....

(7) Write the year given below in Spanish.

1971   ....

La comida y las bebidas

Use **comer** (to eat) and **beber** (to drink) to talk about eating and drinking in Spanish. Make sure you know the different forms of both these verbs before you begin.

1 Fill in the Spanish words on the chart. Remember to put **el, la, los,** or **las** before each one. **Note:** You may use a dictionary to help you.

English	Spanish
rice	
meat	
pasta	
bread	
fruit	
cheese	
eggs	
butter	
fish	
soup	
vegetables	
potatoes	
cake	
ice-cream	

2 Unscramble the Spanish sentences below. Then translate them into English.

queso? quieres ¿ Tú ....

pan? ¿ Tú quieres ....

Time filler:
Keep a food diary in Spanish for a day, or even a week. Use the past tense, beginning your sentences with **Yo comí...** (I ate...) and **Yo bebí...** (I drank...).

(3) Unscramble these Spanish words to reveal a list of drinks.

al echel .... le guaa ....

le afcé .... al malanodi ....

el rocrefse .... el ét ....

el etoochlac .... le muzo de janaran ....

(4) Complete these sentences, using the correct Spanish translation of the English word given in brackets.

¿Vosotros tenéis .... ? (rice)   Yo voy a tomar .... (cereals)

¿Vosotros tenéis .... ? (oil)   Yo voy a tomar .... (jam)

(5) Fill in the gaps in these sentences to describe what you usually eat in a day.

Para mi desayuno yo como ....
.... Yo bebo ....

Para mi almuerzo yo como ....
.... Yo bebo ....

Para mi cena yo como ....
.... Yo bebo ....

En el café

Knowing how to order your favourite snacks and ice-cream flavours in Spanish is a skill that could prove to be useful!

1 Look at the Spanish words for various popular snacks and drinks in the box below. Then find them in the word-search puzzle.

bolsa de patatas	chocolate caliente	trozo de pizza
perrito caliente	bocadillo de queso	hamburguesa
helado	batido	mirinda	pan

b	z	m	k	t	r	o	z	o	d	e	p	i	z	z	a	h
o	d	a	s	d	f	g	h	j	k	l	e	w	f	r	y	b
c	v	c	u	a	b	o	q	p	h	j	r	z	o	w	m	o
a	b	h	e	l	a	d	o	i	z	v	r	x	p	d	l	l
d	n	e	k	x	t	p	e	o	f	c	i	c	a	c	p	s
i	m	t	y	s	i	k	w	u	y	r	t	v	n	v	o	a
l	d	g	h	r	d	l	y	i	q	w	o	b	m	f	i	d
l	q	m	r	a	o	l	w	k	o	r	c	r	k	r	i	e
o	e	i	a	s	f	g	h	j	k	l	a	t	g	t	y	p
d	t	r	z	c	v	x	b	n	m	l	l	y	o	g	u	a
e	y	i	c	o	g	l	a	c	e	m	i	u	r	b	j	t
q	u	n	v	i	q	r	f	o	v	b	e	i	a	n	m	a
u	i	d	d	u	a	d	h	c	d	a	n	o	n	y	t	t
e	o	a	e	h	z	e	o	a	u	i	t	k	g	w	r	a
s	p	k	z	x	c	v	b	g	t	c	e	b	i	n	m	s
o	h	a	m	b	u	r	g	u	e	s	a	o	n	p	k	y
c	h	o	c	o	l	a	t	e	c	a	l	i	e	n	t	e

Time filler:
Spain is famous for its delicious tapas and paella. What other types of food is Spain famous for? Try to write as long a list as you can. Use the Internet to help you.

2 Translate these sentences into English.

¿La carta, por favor? ....

¿Habéis elegido? ....

¿Qué queréis? ....

¿La cuenta, por favor? ....

3 Unscramble these food orders.

una por patatas fritas, Yo favor. ración de quiero

....

queso, Yo favor. por bocadillo quiero de un

....

quiero Yo de trozo un por pizza, favor.

....

batido, favor. un Yo por quiero

....

4 Draw lines to match these ice-cream flavours with their English translations.

un helado de chocolate   a strawberry ice-cream

un helado de grosella   a vanilla ice-cream

un helado de fresa   a blackcurrant ice-cream

un helado de vainilla   a chocolate ice-cream

El cuerpo

When learning the Spanish words for parts of the body, look out for one or two irregular plurals. Can you spot them?

1 Fill in the missing letters in these Spanish words for parts of the body.
Note: You may use a dictionary to help you.

los br__zos	la esp__lda	las orej__s	la g__rganta
las ma__os	el c__ello	la bo__a	los hom__ros
los oj__s	la cab__z a	los p__es	las rod__llas

2 Look at the monkey. Add numbers to the list next to it to say how many of each body part the monkey has.

.... orejas   .... espalda

.... ojos   .... boca

.... manos   .... pies

.... piernas   .... nariz

.... brazos   .... cabeza

.... estómago   .... cola

3 **Me duele el**, or the plural **me duelen los…** can be translated as "I have a pain in…". Choose the right article (**el, la, los** or **las**) to complete these sentences about bodily aches and pains.

Me duelen .... dientes.   Me duele .... estómago.

Me duelen .... ojos.   Me duele .... cabeza.

Me duele .... oreja.   Me duele .... espalda.

Time filler:
Create your own monster! Draw a picture of it and colour it in. Now describe your monster in Spanish. How many heads does it have? How many arms? How many eyes and how many legs? What colour is it?

4 Find the Spanish word for each English clue to complete the crossword puzzle below.

Across

1. hands ....
2. teeth ....
3. ears ....
4. mouth ....
5. knees ....

Down

1. eyes ....
2. body ....
3. fingers ....
4. stomach ....
5. feet ....
6. nose ....
7. legs ....

Las vacaciones

Try using the past tense to talk about what you did on holiday. Just as in English, in Spanish there are different types of past tense. In the exercises below, you will need to use the **pretérito** (the perfect tense) to say what happened to you.

1 Translate these sentences into Spanish.

I travelled by plane. ....

He travelled by car. ....

We travelled by boat. ....

2 Translate these sentences into Spanish.

Pierre went to Italy. ....

Sophie went to France. ....

My sisters went to Africa. ....

My parents went to Portugal. ....

3 Choose the correct form of the perfect tense of **ir** (to go) to complete these sentences.

Nosotros .... a una iglesia.

Él .... a un castillo.

Ellas .... a la playa.

Vosotros .... al museo.

Yo ...... a un lago.

Time filler:
Getting ready to go on a holiday is always fun. What do you need to buy before you go? Make a list in Spanish to take with you when you go shopping. Start it with **Voy a comprar...** (I am going to buy...).

4 Here are some useful Spanish expressions to help you say what you thought about some of the things you did on holiday. Draw lines to match them to their English translations.

Fue divertido.   It was dull.

Fue pesado.   It was frightening.

Fue rápido.   It was great!

¡Fue apasionante!   It was funny.

Fue terrorífico.   It was fast.

¡Fue genial!   It was exciting!

5 You may have visited an amusement park while on holiday. Choose the correct form of the perfect tense of **ver** (to see) to complete these sentences and say what your family saw on the ghost-train ride. Then write the English translation.

Mi hermana .... un hombre lobo.

....

Mi hermano .... un vampiro.

....

Mis padres .... unas arañas.

....

Yo .... un esqueleto.

....

Beat the clock 3

Write the correct present tense form of the verbs shown in brackets below. Remember that they are all regular verbs that end in **-ar**. **¡Vamos!**

Yo (hablar) ....

Tú (pasar) ....

Él (quedar) ....

Nosotros (hablar) ....

Ellos (pasar) ....

Ella (llamar) ....

Yo (mirar) ....

Nosotros (mirar) ....

Yo (entrar) ....

Él (trabajar) ....

Tú (tomar) ....

Ella (pasar) ....

Nosotros (comprar) ....

Ellas (llamar) ....

Ella (quedar) ....

Él (llamar) ....

Tú (hablar) ....

Yo (pasar) ....

Ellos (quedar) ....

Ellos (llamar) ....

Tú (mirar) ....

Vosotros (hablar) ....

Tú (entrar) ....

Él (tomar) ....

Tú (comprar) ....

Yo (trabajar) ....

Vosotros (mirar) ....

Yo (quedar) ....

Él (hablar) ....

Nosotros (pasar) ....

Tú (quedar) ....

Vosotros (llamar) ....

Él (mirar) ....

Él (entrar) ....

Ella (tomar) ....

Ellas (hablar) ....

Nosotros (llamar) ....

Tú (trabajar) ....

Él comprar ....

Ellos (mirar) ....

Ellas (pasar) ....

Nosotros (quedar) ....

Yo (llamar) ....

Él (pasar) ....

Ella (mirar) ....

Ella (hablar) ....

Vosotros (quedar) ....

Ellas (mirar) ....

Tú (llamar) ....

Ellos (hablar) ....

Vosotros (pasar) ....

Ella (entrar) ....

Nosotros (tomar) ....

Él (trabajar) ....

Vosotros (comprar) ....

Ellas (quedar) ....

Answers:

04–05 ¡Hola! ¿Cómo estás?
06–07 Los números 1–20

4

1. **Buenos días** means "good morning" and the more informal **hola** can be translated as "hello" or "hi". Write the best greeting for each of these people.

your friend _____hola_____   a policeman _____buenos días_____

your teacher _____buenos días_____   your mother _____hola_____

2. Here are three Spanish expressions that you might use to say how you feel. Draw lines to match each one to a picture below.

Mal.   Normal.   Bien, gracias.

3. To be polite, use **señor** (sir), **señora** (madam) and **señorita** (miss) with your greetings. Say **adiós** (goodbye) politely to the people in these pictures.

¡Adiós, señorita!   ¡Adiós, señor!   ¡Adiós, señora!

5

4. Here are two ways of asking "What is your name?" in Spanish, but the vowels are missing. Add the vowels to complete each sentence.

¿Cómo te llamas?

¿Cuál es tu nombre?

5. Match each Spanish name with its English equivalent.

Juan   Pedro   María   Carlos   Lucía

Mary   John   Lucy   Peter   Charles

6. Translate each phrase from English to Spanish. Use the Spanish equivalent of people's names.

Goodbye, John!   ¡Adiós, Juan!
My name is Mary.   Me llamo María.
How are you, Lucy?   ¿Cómo estás, Lucía?

7. The words in these greetings are all mixed up. Unscramble them and write each sentence correctly.

gracias. Bien,   Bien, gracias.
te llamas? ¿Cómo   ¿Cómo te llamas?
señora! ¡Buenos días,   ¡Buenos días, señora!

The activities on these pages give practice in making basic introductions in Spanish. Make sure that as well as giving answers, your child practises asking simple questions. When asking a question, encourage your child to raise his or her voice at the beginning. Ensure that he or she uses the polite form **Buenos días** and **señor, señora** or **señorita,** to greet people in more formal situations.

6

1. A rocket is about to be launched. Below is the countdown in Spanish, but some of the numbers are missing. Fill in the gaps.

diez, nueve, _ocho_, siete, _seis_, _cinco_, cuatro, _tres_, _dos_, _uno_, cero! Fuego!

2. Write the number for each Spanish number word.

uno _1_   dos _2_   cuatro _4_
siete _7_   ocho _8_   diez _10_
once _11_   doce _12_   trece _13_
quince _15_   diecisiete _17_   veinte _20_

3. Complete each calculation in Spanish.

diez + siete = _diecisiete_   ocho + dos = _diez_
cinco + siete = _doce_   doce – uno = _once_
tres x dos = _seis_   veinte – cinco = _quince_

4. Circle the even numbers.

uno   (cuatro)   (doce)   once   diecisiete

7

5. Translate each number into Spanish. Then complete the crossword.

Across
1. two _dos_
2. eleven _once_
3. three _tres_
4. twelve _doce_
5. nine _nueve_

Down
1. eight _ocho_
2. twenty _veinte_
3. ten _diez_
4. seven _siete_
5. thirteen _trece_

It is a good idea to keep revisiting numbers. Children may find it helpful to try saying numbers in Spanish whenever they notice them around the house, or when they are out and about. Your child can also try using Spanish numbers in games with simple scores or games involving dice.

Answers:

08–09 Mi familia
10–11 ¿Cuántos años tienes?

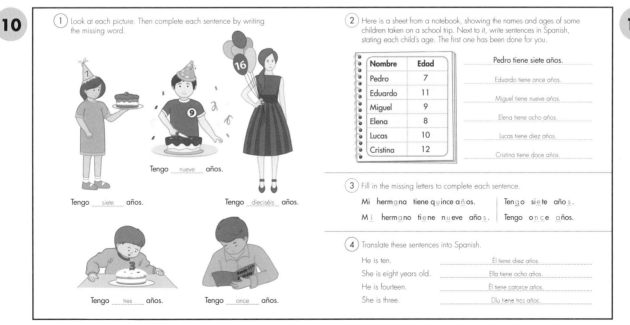

8

1) Read the information given in the chart below. Then use it to write the name of the child shown in each picture.

Me llamo Alfonso. Tengo una hermana y un hermano.	Me llamo Sofía. Tengo dos hermanos.
Me llamo Elena. Tengo una hermana. No tengo un hermano.	Me llamo José. No tengo ni hermanos ni hermanas.

José

Elena

Sofía

Alfonso

2) Translate these phrases. Remember to use the correct Spanish word for "my" (**mi** or **mis**) in each case.

my brothers ___mis hermanos___   my mother ___mi madre___
my grandmother ___mi abuela___   my sisters ___mis hermanas___

9

3) Look at the people in this family. Then complete each sentence.

Cristina   Andrés   Nuria   José María
Juan   Luis
David   Silvia

El padre se llama… ___José María___   La madre se llama… ___Cristina___
El abuelo se llama… ___Andrés___   La abuela se llama… ___Nuria___
El niño pequeño se llama… ___David___   La hermana se llama… ___Silvia___
Los bebés se llaman… ___Luis y Juan___
Los niños se llaman… ___David, Silvia, Luis y Juan___

4) Circle the correct form of the verb **llamarse** (to be called) in each sentence.

Mis hermanos se llama /(se llaman) Adrián y Carlos.

La hermana de David (se llama)/ se llaman Elena.

Mis padres se llama /(se llaman) Lucas y María.

By working through this page, your child will be motivated to write about their family and friends. Children will enjoy using authentic Spanish names, which they can find on the internet. Point out the different verb endings for **llamarse**. Ask how the spelling changes when talking about one person or more than one person – we need to add **a** or **an**, respectively.

10

1) Look at each picture. Then complete each sentence by writing the missing word.

Tengo ___nueve___ años.

Tengo ___siete___ años.

Tengo ___dieciséis___ años.

Tengo ___tres___ años.

Tengo ___once___ años.

11

2) Here is a sheet from a notebook, showing the names and ages of some children taken on a school trip. Next to it, write sentences in Spanish, stating each child's age. The first one has been done for you.

Nombre	Edad
Pedro	7
Eduardo	11
Miguel	9
Elena	8
Lucas	10
Cristina	12

Pedro tiene siete años.
Eduardo tiene once años.
Miguel tiene nueve años.
Elena tiene ocho años.
Lucas tiene diez años.
Cristina tiene doce años.

3) Fill in the missing letters to complete each sentence.

Mi herm**a**na tiene q**u**ince año**s**.   Teng**o** si**e**te año**s**.
M**i** herm**a**no ti**e**ne n**u**eve año**s**.   Tengo o**n**ce **a**ños.

4) Translate these sentences into Spanish.

He is ten. ___Él tiene diez años.___
She is eight years old. ___Ella tiene ocho años.___
He is fourteen. ___Él tiene catorce años.___
She is three. ___Ella tiene tres años.___

Your child needs to practise the question form – **¿Cuántos años tienes?** – as well as ways to reply. Point out the use of accents on letters in Spanish words, such as **á** in cuántos and **ñ** in **años**. It is helpful for your child to be aware from the start that accents can change sounds and are an important part of the correct spelling of a word.

Answers:

12–13 En mi mochila
14–15 Los números 20–69

12

1 Fill in the chart. Add the Spanish word for each object listed in English, as well as the correct Spanish word for "the" (**el** or **la**) that you would use in each case. **Note:** You may use a dictionary to help you.

English	el or la	Spanish
pencil	el	lápiz
pen	el	bolígrafo
rubber	la	goma
pencil case	el	estuche
calculator	la	calculadora
felt-tip pen	el	rotulador
pencil sharpener	el	sacapuntas
school bag	la	mochila
notebook	el	cuaderno
ruler	la	regla

2 Circle the correct Spanish word for "a/an" in each phrase.

un /(una) bolsa   un /(una) regla
un /(una) goma   (un)/ una lápiz
(un)/ una bolígrafo   (un)/ una estuche
(un)/ una rotulador   un /(una) calculadora
(un)/ una cuaderno   (un)/ una sacapuntas

13

3 The following sentence is written as a code.

7 1   18 14   18 15 26 3 14 2 4   9 7 1 11 15 25 1 4   6 7 11 2 4.

Use this code-breaking chart to reveal what letter each number in the coded sentence stands for. Then write the decoded message.

a	b	c	e	g	h	i	l	m	n	o	r	s	t	u	y
4	17	26	7	11	3	14	2	18	1	15	6	23	9	25	13

En mi mochila, tengo una regla.

4 Find the Spanish words for ten classroom objects in this word-search puzzle. **Hint:** All the words can be found on the chart on page 12.

(word search grid)

These pages provide a good opportunity to talk about the gender of nouns. Explain that the Spanish words for "a/an" and "the" will change depending on whether they are followed by a masculine, feminine or plural noun.

14

1 Complete each number word in the chart.

Number	Number word
23	veinti trés
34	treinta y cuatro
41	cuarenta y uno
52	cincuenta y dos
69	sesenta y nueve

2 Write these numbers as digits.

treinta y uno 31   sesenta y siete 67   veinticuatro 24
veintiséis 26   cincuenta y ocho 58   cuarenta y nueve 49

3 Write the Spanish for each number.

51 cincuenta y uno   42 cuarenta y dos   63 sesenta y tres
29 veintinueve   35 treinta y cinco   57 cincuenta y siete

4 Write the next two numbers in each sequence.

veintiuno, veintidós… veintitrés, veinticuatro
cuarenta y seis, cuarenta y siete…. cuarenta y ocho, cuarenta y nueve

15

5 Solve these sums. Write the answers, first in digits and then in Spanish.

3 x 7 = 21 veintiuno   6 x 7 = 42 cuarenta y dos
9 x 3 = 27 veintisiete   12 x 3 = 36 treinta y seis
6 x 8 = 48 cuarenta y ocho   10 x 5 = 50 cincuenta
8 x 8 = 64 sesenta y cuatro   11 x 5 = 55 cincuenta y cinco
7 x 9 = 63 sesenta y tres   11 x 3 = 33 treinta y tres

6 In this word-search puzzle, find the Spanish words for the ten numbers that are answers to the sums in question 5.

(word search grid)

For numbers such as 31 and 41, children will need a reminder to include **y**, which helps with pronunciation. For example, the Spanish for 31 is **treinta y uno**. Numbers need lots of reinforcement. Your child may enjoy counting games in Spanish. For example, try clapping a number of times, then ask your child to tell you in Spanish how many times you've clapped.

Answers:

16–17 Los meses del año
18–19 Los adjetivos
20–21 Beat the clock 1, see p.80

16

(1) Select Spanish words for the months of the year from the chart below to match the list of months in English.

agosto	enero	septiembre	marzo	noviembre	abril
febrero	mayo	junio	octubre	diciembre	julio

January   enero   July   julio
February   febrero   August   agosto
March   marzo   September   septiembre
April   abril   October   octubre
May   mayo   November   noviembre
June   junio   December   diciembre

(2) Use the first letter and the number of spaces provided as clues to work out the birthday month of each child.

Mi cumpleaños es el 26 de e n e r o.

Mi cumpleaños es el 17 de a b r i l.

Mi cumpleaños es el 10 de f e b r e r o.

Mi cumpleaños es el 31 de m a y o.

17

(3) ¿Cuándo es tu cumpleaños?
When is your birthday? Answers may vary

(4) The letters have fallen out of the bottom of this puzzle grid! On the way down, they got mixed up, although they are still in their correct rows. Unscramble them to discover the mystery birthday date.

			m	i						
c	u	m	p	l	e	a	ñ	o	s	
			e	s			e	l		
v	e	i	n	t	i	u	n	o		d e
s	e	p	t	i	e	m	b	r	e	

i m
m u l c ñ s a o e p
s e e l
n i t e n i o v u e d
m e e t b p r s e i

(5) Continue this sequence.

marzo   abril   mayo   junio   julio   agosto

It is a good idea to start by asking children what month their birthday is in and then progress to combining numbers and months. Your child may enjoy keeping a small birthday book in Spanish, where he or she records the birthdays of family and friends. Keep reminding your child that in Spanish, months begin with a lower-case letter, unlike in English.

18

(1) Write the feminine form and the English translation for each adjective listed on the chart. **Note:** You may use a dictionary to help you.

Spanish (Masculine)	Spanish (Feminine)	English
bueno	buena	good
tímido	tímida	shy
glotón	glotona	greedy
pequeño	pequeña	small
grande	grande	big
deportista	deportista	sporty
malo	mala	naughty
bonito	bonita	beautiful
perezoso	perezosa	lazy
amable	amable	kind/friendly
divertido	divertida	funny
simpático	simpática	nice

(2) Complete the following sentences using adjectives from the chart above.

Soy   Answers may vary   y   Answers may vary .

Mi madre es   Answers may vary   y   Answers may vary .

19

(3) Choose your favourite character from a book or a film. Write a few sentences describing him or her in Spanish. Answers may vary

(4) Circle the adjective in each Spanish sentence that correctly matches the English sentences.

He has brown hair.   Él tiene el pelo (marrón) / rojo / rubio / negro.

She has red hair.   Ella tiene el pelo marrón / (rojo) / rubio / negro.

He has green eyes.   Él tiene los ojos marrones / azules / (verdes) / grises.

She has blue eyes.   Ella tiene los ojos marrones / (azules) / verdes / grises.

(5) Write a brief description of yourself in Spanish. Use **Soy**... (I am...) and **Tengo**... (I have...) to begin your sentences. Answers may vary

Once children know about the gender of nouns, they can begin using adjectives, which need to agree with nouns. Ask your child to tell you how the spelling of masculine and feminine adjectives change. Explain that for a feminine adjective, the **-o** at the end of the masculine form often changes to **-a**. Point out that the masculine and feminine forms of adjectives ending in **-e** or **ista** are the same.

70

Answers:

22–23 Los colores
24–25 Los días de la semana

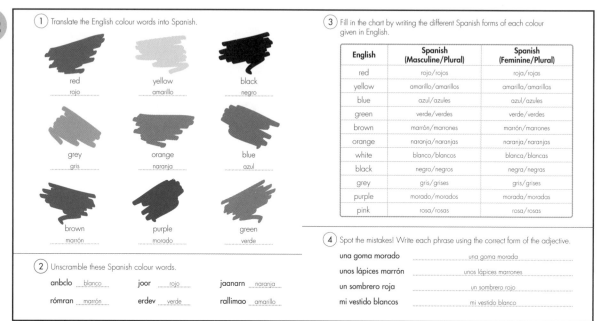

22

① Translate the English colour words into Spanish.

red — rojo
yellow — amarillo
black — negro
grey — gris
orange — naranja
blue — azul
brown — marrón
purple — morado
green — verde

② Unscramble these Spanish colour words.

anbclo — blanco   joor — rojo   jaanarn — naranja

rómran — marrón   erdev — verde   rallimao — amarillo

23

③ Fill in the chart by writing the different Spanish forms of each colour given in English.

English	Spanish (Masculine/Plural)	Spanish (Feminine/Plural)
red	rojo/rojos	roja/rojas
yellow	amarillo/amarillos	amarilla/amarillas
blue	azul/azules	azul/azules
green	verde/verdes	verde/verdes
brown	marrón/marrones	marrón/marrones
orange	naranja/naranjas	naranja/naranjas
white	blanco/blancos	blanca/blancas
black	negro/negros	negra/negras
grey	gris/grises	gris/grises
purple	morado/morados	morada/moradas
pink	rosa/rosas	rosa/rosas

④ Spot the mistakes! Write each phrase using the correct form of the adjective.

una goma morado — una goma morada
unos lápices marrón — unos lápices marrones
un sombrero roja — un sombrero rojo
mi vestido blancos — mi vestido blanco

Remind your child that colours are adjectives and they need to agree with the noun they describe. This could mean using masculine, feminine, masculine plural or feminine plural. Point out that unlike in English, Spanish colours go after the noun. Your child will need to watch out for invariable adjectives, such as **naranja** or **azul**, where the spelling remains the same.

24

① Draw a line linking each day in Spanish to its English equivalent.

martes — Sunday
sábado — Monday
jueves — Tuesday
lunes — Wednesday
miércoles — Thursday
domingo — Friday
viernes — Saturday

② Continue each sequence.

martes — miércoles — jueves — viernes

viernes — sábado — domingo — lunes

domingo — lunes — martes — miércoles

miércoles — jueves — viernes — sábado

25

③ Complete these sentences.

Antes del martes, es lunes.

Después del sábado, es domingo.

Antes del viernes, es jueves.

Después del lunes, es martes.

④ Translate the following dates into Spanish.

Monday, 3rd July — lunes, 3 de julio

Saturday, 1st September — sábado, 1 de septiembre

Wednesday, 5th January — miércoles, 5 de enero

⑤ Answer the questions in Spanish. Answers may vary

What is the date tomorrow?

What was the date yesterday?

What will the date be in two days' time?

Encourage your child to keep a simple diary in Spanish, using a page for each week. Divide each page into seven sections and write the days in Spanish. Your child could draw pictures and use simple Spanish phrases to remind him or her about what is happening each day. Make sure your child uses lower-case initial letters for the months and days of the week.

Answers:

26–27 Los animales
28–29 La casa

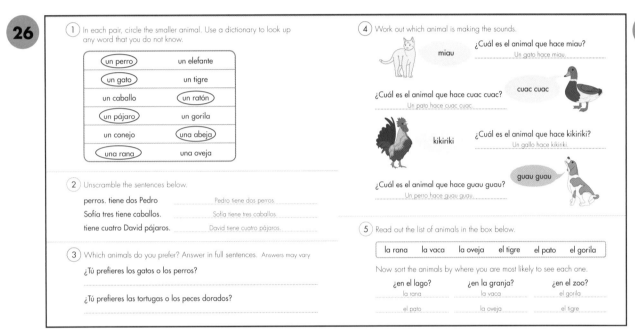

26

1. In each pair, circle the smaller animal. Use a dictionary to look up any word that you do not know.

(un perro) — un elefante
(un gato) — un tigre
un caballo — (un ratón)
(un pájaro) — un gorila
un conejo — (una abeja)
(una rana) — una oveja

2. Unscramble the sentences below.

perros. tiene dos Pedro — Pedro tiene dos perros.
Sofía tres tiene caballos. — Sofía tiene tres caballos.
tiene cuatro David pájaros. — David tiene cuatro pájaros.

3. Which animals do you prefer? Answer in full sentences. Answers may vary

¿Tú prefieres los gatos o los perros?

¿Tú prefieres las tortugas o los peces dorados?

27

4. Work out which animal is making the sounds.

miau — ¿Cuál es el animal que hace miau? — Un gato hace miau.

¿Cuál es el animal que hace cuac cuac? — Un pato hace cuac cuac. — cuac cuac

kikiriki — ¿Cuál es el animal que hace kikiriki? — Un gallo hace kikiriki.

¿Cuál es el animal que hace guau guau? — Un perro hace guau guau. — guau guau

5. Read out the list of animals in the box below.

| la rana | la vaca | la oveja | el tigre | el pato | el gorila |

Now sort the animals by where you are most likely to see each one.

¿en el lago?	¿en la granja?	¿en el zoo?
la rana	la vaca	el gorila
el pato	la oveja	el tigre

Talking about animals is a good opportunity for your child to practise the verb **tener**. For example, **Sofía tiene tres caballos.** Refer to pages 10, 13 and 18, where your child also makes use of **yo tengo, él tiene** and **ella tiene**. Also ask him or her what they notice about plural spellings in this section. Use a dictionary to look up the Spanish words for different animals, taking note of any irregular plurals.

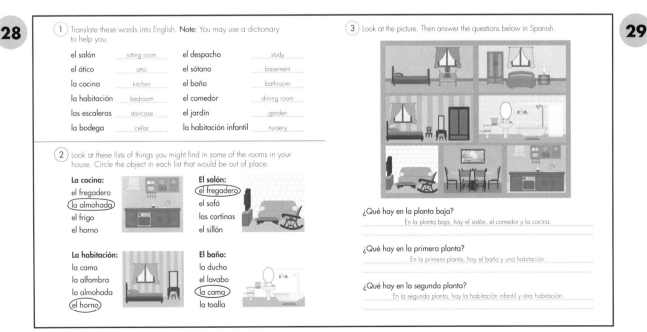

28

1. Translate these words into English. **Note:** You may use a dictionary to help you.

el salón — sitting room
el ático — attic
la cocina — kitchen
la habitación — bedroom
las escaleras — staircase
la bodega — cellar
el despacho — study
el sótano — basement
el baño — bathroom
el comedor — dining room
el jardín — garden
la habitación infantil — nursery

2. Look at these lists of things you might find in some of the rooms in your house. Circle the object in each list that would be out of place.

La cocina:
el fregadero
(la almohada)
el frigo
el horno

El salón:
(el fregadero)
el sofá
las cortinas
el sillón

La habitación:
la cama
la alfombra
la almohada
(el horno)

El baño:
la ducha
el lavabo
(la cama)
la toalla

29

3. Look at the picture. Then answer the questions below in Spanish.

¿Qué hay en la planta baja?
En la planta baja, hay el salón, el comedor y la cocina.

¿Qué hay en la primera planta?
En la primera planta, hay el baño y una habitación.

¿Qué hay en la segunda planta?
En la segunda planta, hay la habitación infantil y otra habitación.

On these pages, your child is encouraged to use a dictionary. Guide your child to use the English-Spanish and Spanish-English sections. Encourage your child to keep a vocabulary book with pages marked with the letters of the alphabet to note down new words he or she has discovered. This activity will help your child to expand his or her Spanish vocabulary gradually.

Answers:

30–31 ¿Dónde vives?
32–33 Los países

30

(1) Complete the chart by adding the English translations.

Spanish	English
una casa	a house
un piso	a flat
una casa pareada	a semi-detached house
un chalet	a detached house
una casa adosada	a terraced house
un bungalow	a bungalow

(2) Find out what the Spanish expressions mean by unscrambling their English translations.

Spanish	English		
en la ciudad	in tnow	=	in town
en el campo	in the cidentrouys	=	in the countryside
en las afueras	in the rbssubu	=	in the suburbs
en las montañas	in the itmounasn	=	in the mountains
en la playa/junto al mar	by the esa	=	by the sea

31

(3) Insert the correct form of the present tense of the verb **vivir** (to live) in these sentences.

Yo _vivo_ en Londres.

Él _vive_ en la playa.

Tú _vives_ en las afueras.

Ellos _viven_ en el campo.

Nosotros _vivimos_ en la ciudad.

Vosotros _vivís_ en un pueblo.

(4) Translate these Spanish sentences into English.

Vivo con mis padres en una casa adosada.
I live with my parents in a terraced house.

Ella vive con su madre en un piso grande.
She lives with her mother in a big flat.

(5) Translate these English sentences into Spanish.

My grandparents live on an old farm in the mountains.
Mis abuelos viven en una granja vieja en las montañas.

My cousins live in a bungalow by the sea.
Mis primos viven en un bungalow junto al mar.

The forms Spanish verbs take are very different from English verbs. This section provides a good opportunity to practise the different endings of an **–ir** verb (**vivir**). Ask your child which letters need to be added to **viv–** for each pronoun (**yo**, **tú**, **él**, **ella**, **nosotros**, **vosotros**, **ellos**, **ellas**).

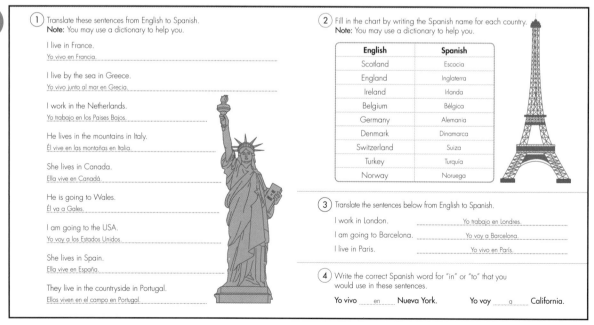

32

(1) Translate these sentences from English to Spanish.
Note: You may use a dictionary to help you.

I live in France.
Yo vivo en Francia.

I live by the sea in Greece.
Yo vivo junto al mar en Grecia.

I work in the Netherlands.
Yo trabajo en los Países Bajos.

He lives in the mountains in Italy.
Él vive en las montañas en Italia.

She lives in Canada.
Ella vive en Canadá.

He is going to Wales.
Él va a Gales.

I am going to the USA.
Yo voy a los Estados Unidos.

She lives in Spain.
Ella vive en España.

They live in the countryside in Portugal.
Ellos viven en el campo en Portugal.

33

(2) Fill in the chart by writing the Spanish name for each country.
Note: You may use a dictionary to help you.

English	Spanish
Scotland	Escocia
England	Inglaterra
Ireland	Irlanda
Belgium	Bélgica
Germany	Alemania
Denmark	Dinamarca
Switzerland	Suiza
Turkey	Turquía
Norway	Noruega

(3) Translate the sentences below from English to Spanish.

I work in London. — Yo trabajo en Londres.
I am going to Barcelona. — Yo voy a Barcelona.
I live in Paris. — Yo vivo en París.

(4) Write the correct Spanish word for "in" or "to" that you would use in these sentences.

Yo vivo _en_ Nueva York.   Yo voy _a_ California.

In this activity, your child will gain practice in using some forms of the irregular verb **ir** – **yo voy** and **él/ella va**. For further practice, children may enjoy building sentences of their own, modelled on the sentences used here. Encourage your child to combine **yo voy/él va/ella va** with different cities and countries.

Answers:

34–35 En la ciudad
36–37 ¿Dónde está…?

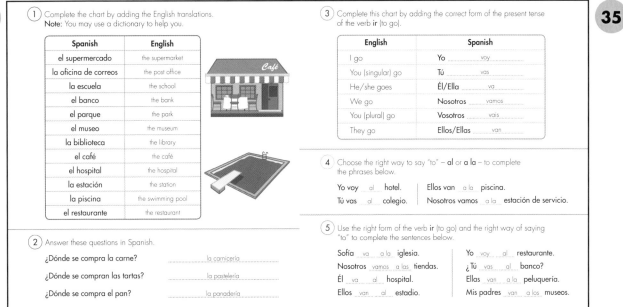

34

1. Complete the chart by adding the English translations.
Note: You may use a dictionary to help you.

Spanish	English
el supermercado	the supermarket
la oficina de correos	the post office
la escuela	the school
el banco	the bank
el parque	the park
el museo	the museum
la biblioteca	the library
el café	the café
el hospital	the hospital
la estación	the station
la piscina	the swimming pool
el restaurante	the restaurant

2. Answer these questions in Spanish.

¿Dónde se compra la carne? .... la carnicería

¿Dónde se compran las tartas? .... la pastelería

¿Dónde se compra el pan? .... la panadería

35

3. Complete this chart by adding the correct form of the present tense of the verb **ir** (to go).

English	Spanish
I go	Yo .... voy
You (singular) go	Tú .... vas
He/she goes	Él/Ella .... va
We go	Nosotros .... vamos
You (plural) go	Vosotros .... vais
They go	Ellos/Ellas .... van

4. Choose the right way to say "to" – **al** or **a la** – to complete the phrases below.

Yo voy ___al___ hotel.   Ellos van ___a la___ piscina.

Tú vas ___al___ colegio.   Nosotros vamos ___a la___ estación de servicio.

5. Use the right form of the verb **ir** (to go) and the right way of saying "to" to complete the sentences below.

Sofía ___va___ ___a la___ iglesia.   Yo ___voy___ ___al___ restaurante.

Nosotros ___vamos___ ___a las___ tiendas.   ¿Tú ___vas___ ___al___ banco?

Él ___va___ ___al___ hospital.   Ellas ___van___ ___a la___ peluquería.

Ellos ___van___ ___al___ estadio.   Mis padres ___van___ ___a los___ museos.

These pages will help your child grasp the use of the verb **ir**. He or she will also begin to use the preposition **a**, which becomes **al**, **a la**, **a los** or **a las** depending on whether the noun that follows it is masculine, feminine, singular or plural.

36

1. Unscramble these sentences to reveal three requests for directions.

¿Cómo llegar puedo a estación? la
¿Cómo puedo llegar a la estación?

Disculpe señora, ir oficina de correos? a la¿ para
Disculpe señora, ¿para ir a la oficina de correos?

Disculpe señor, el¿ dónde está restaurante?
Disculpe señor, ¿dónde está el restaurante?

2. Draw lines linking the Spanish phrases with their English translations.

enfrente de — in front of
cerca de — near
entre — between
al lado de — next to
delante de — opposite
detrás de — behind

3. Choose from **del**, **de la**, **de los** or **de las** to complete the directions below.

Hay una oficina de correos enfrente ___de la___ estación.

Hay un banco cerca ___del___ hotel.

Hay una oficina de turismo cerca ___de las___ tiendas.

37

4. Translate these English sentences into Spanish.

The bank is between the church and the museum.
El banco está entre la iglesia y el museo.

My school is near my house and the park.
Mi escuela está cerca de mi casa y del parque.

The library is next to the café and the station.
La biblioteca está al lado del café y de la estación.

5. Look at these symbols for various directions.

Siga todo recto

Gire a la derecha

Gire a la izquierda

Coja la segunda calle a la derecha

Coja la primera calle a la izquierda

Now write in Spanish what the sequences of symbols below mean:

Siga todo recto y coja la segunda calle a la derecha.

Coja la primera calle a la izquierda y gire a la derecha.

Siga todo recto y gire a la izquierda.

In this section, your child will practise three different model sentences to ask for directions. He or she will also need to choose the correct form – **del**, **de la**, **de los** or **de las** – to complete directions, depending on whether the noun that follows is masculine, feminine, singular or plural.

Answers:

38–39 El tiempo libre
40–41 ¿Qué hora es?
42–43 Beat the clock 2, see p.80

38

1 Fill in the chart by ticking (✔) the correct column to say which of the sports listed is masculine or feminine, and adding the English translation.
Note: You may use a dictionary to help you.

Spanish	Masculine	Feminine	English
tenis	✔		tennis
fútbol	✔		football
equitación		✔	horseriding
natación		✔	swimming
gimnasia		✔	gymnastics
esquí	✔		skiing
windsurf	✔		windsurfing

2 Use the correct form of the verb **practicar** (to practise) to complete the sentences below.

Yo _practico_ el esquí.
Nosotros _practicamos_ la equitación.
Tú _practicas_ la natación.
Él _practica_ la gimnasia.

39

3 Write the correct form of **jugar al/a la** or **practicar** to complete each sentence.

Ellas _practican_ el patinaje.
Tú _juegas al_ tenis.
Nosotros _jugamos al_ fútbol.
Yo _practico_ la natación.
Él _practica_ la gimnasia.
Vosotros _jugáis al_ rugby.

4 Write about which sports you like and which you dislike by completing the following sentences. Answers may vary

Me gusta _____ .
No me gusta _____ .
Me encanta _____ .
Yo odio _____ .
Mi deporte favorito es _____ .

5 Choose the correct verb from the box below to complete the sentences.

escuchar	ir	montar	leer

Me gusta _montar_ en bici.
Me gusta _leer_ los libros.
Me gusta _ir_ a las tiendas.
Me gusta _escuchar_ la música.

Here your child will practise the useful model phrase **Me gusta** + an infinitive verb. Encourage your child to build further sentences of his or her own using this model, saying that he or she enjoys doing a variety of different activities.

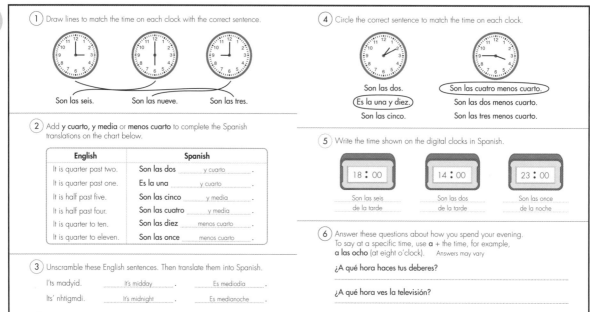

40

1 Draw lines to match the time on each clock with the correct sentence.

Son las seis. Son las nueve. Son las tres.

2 Add **y cuarto, y media** or **menos cuarto** to complete the Spanish translations on the chart below.

English	Spanish
It is quarter past two.	Son las dos _y cuarto_ .
It is quarter past one.	Es la una _y cuarto_ .
It is half past five.	Son las cinco _y media_ .
It is half past four.	Son las cuatro _y media_ .
It is quarter to ten.	Son las diez _menos cuarto_ .
It is quarter to eleven.	Son las once _menos cuarto_ .

3 Unscramble these English sentences. Then translate them into Spanish.

I'ts madyid. _It's midday_ . _Es mediodía_ .
Its' nhtigmdi. _It's midnight_ . _Es medianoche_ .

41

4 Circle the correct sentence to match the time on each clock.

Son las dos.
(Es la una y diez.)
Son las cinco.

(Son las cuatro menos cuarto.)
Son las dos menos cuarto.
Son las tres menos cuarto.

5 Write the time shown on the digital clocks in Spanish.

18 : 00 — Son las seis de la tarde
14 : 00 — Son las dos de la tarde
23 : 00 — Son las once de la noche

6 Answer these questions about how you spend your evening. To say at a specific time, use **a** + the time, for example, **a las ocho** (at eight o'clock). Answers may vary

¿A qué hora haces tus deberes? _____

¿A qué hora ves la televisión? _____

Before starting these activities, it is a good idea to reinforce the numbers 1 to 12. Your child might struggle to use the correct hour when using **menos cuarto**. First, make sure he or she understands which hour the long hand is approaching. Then remind him or her that for any time other than one o'clock, the plural form **Son las...** (It is...) will need to be used.

Answers:

44–45 Mi rutina
46–47 La ropa

44

1 Choose reflexive pronouns from the box below to complete the different forms of the present tense of the verb **levantarse** (to get up).

se	me	te	os	nos

Yo __me__ levanto.   Nosotros __nos__ levantamos.
Tú __te__ levantas.   Vosotros __os__ levantáis.
Él/Ella __se__ levanta.   Ellos/Ellas __se__ levantan.

2 Draw lines to match the Spanish sentences about your daily routine to their English translation.

Yo me levanto. — I wake up.
Yo me despierto. — I get dressed.
Yo me peino. — I get up.
Yo me ducho. — I comb my hair.
Yo me acuesto. — I brush my teeth.
Yo me visto. — I have a shower.
Yo me lavo los dientes. — I go to bed.
Yo como/almuerzo. — I read a book.
Yo leo un libro. — I have lunch.

45

3 Write the English for these Spanish adverbs. **Note:** You may use a dictionary to help you.

normalmente .... usually
a menudo .... often
de vez en cuando .... from time to time
raramente .... seldom

4 Complete the following sentences by adding an adverb to say how often you do the after-school activities mentioned.   Answers may vary

Yo leo ....
Yo salgo con mis amigos ....
Yo veo la televisión ....
Yo hago mis deberes ....
Yo escucho la música ....

5 Read the paragraph in Spanish below. Underline the time-connective words and phrases.

En primer lugar, yo me despierto. Habitualmente me levanto cinco minutos más tarde. Luego, me lavo, me visto y tomo mi desayuno. Después, me lavo los dientes. Finalmente, me peino.

Explain to your child that reflexive verbs describe actions that you do to yourself. They follow the same rules as other **–ar**, **–er** and **–ir** verbs for conjugation, but they also have a reflexive pronoun (**me**, **te**, **se**, **nos** or **os**) in front of the verb.

46

1 Fill the gaps on the chart below. Use a dictionary to look up new words.

Spanish	English	Spanish	English
unos pantalones	trousers	una camisa	a shirt
unos vaqueros	jeans	un vestido	a dress
una camiseta	a T-shirt	una falda	a skirt
una blusa	a blouse	una bufanda	a scarf
un abrigo	a coat	unos guantes	gloves
un gorro	a hat	unos calcetines	socks
un pijama	pyjamas	unos zapatos	shoes
unos pantalones cortos	shorts	unas sandalias	sandals

2 Discover what people are wearing by using the code-breaking key to decipher the sentences below.

e = ♠   u = ♥   o = ♣   a = ♦   s = ☼

N♥ri♦ ll♦v♦ ♥n v♦☼tid♣ y ♥n♦☼ ☼♦nd♦li♦☼.
Nuria lleva un vestido y unas sandalias.

♦l♦n♦ ll♦v♦ ♥n♦ f♦ld♦ y ♥n♦ bl♥☼♦.
Elena lleva una falda y una blusa.

T♣m ll♦v♦ ♥n♣☼ p♦nt♦l♦n♦☼ c♦rt♦☼ y ♥n♦ c♦mi☼♦t♦.
Tom lleva unos pantalones cortos y una camiseta.

47

3 In each box, draw a picture of the garment described in Spanish. Drawings may vary

una bufanda roja de lunares | un vestido rosa a cuadros | una camiseta blanca a rayas verdes | una falda azul de flores

4 Finish these sentences. Note the use of the past tense (Yo llevé/I wore) and the near future tense (Voy a llevar/I am going to wear).

Hoy, yo llevo .... Answers may vary ....
Ayer, yo llevé .... Answers may vary ....
Mañana, voy a llevar .... Answers may vary ....

5 Complete these sentences by describing what outfit you will wear.

Para ir al pueblo, yo voy a llevar .... Answers may vary ....
Para ir a la playa, yo voy a llevar .... Answers may vary ....

Describing clothes will give your child lots of opportunities to practise adjectival agreement. Encourage your child to refer back to pages 18–19 and 22–23. Also remind him or her that colours need to follow the noun. On these pages your child is also introduced to the past tense **yo llevé** (I wore) and the near future tense **yo voy a llevar** (I am going to wear).

Answers:

48–49 ¿Qué tiempo hace?
50–51 En la escuela

48

1 Fill in the missing letters in the Spanish descriptions of the weather symbols. **Note:** You may use a dictionary to help you.

Está llov**i e n d o**.   Es**t á** nubl**a d o**.

Está nev**a n d o**.   Ha**y** tor**m e n** ta.

Ha**c** ce **ca l** or.   Ha**c**ce **v i e** nto.

Ha**c**ce **f r í o**.   Ha**c**ce **s o l**.

2 Describe the weather during the different seasons of the year by filling in the gaps in these sentences. The first one has been done for you.

En invierno, _____nieva_____ y _____hace frío_____ .

En primavera, ___Answers may vary___ y ___Answers may vary___ .

En verano, ___Answers may vary___ y ___Answers may vary___ .

En otoño, ___Answers may vary___ y ___Answers may vary___ .

49

3 Complete these sentences, writing what you would wear for the weather described.   Answers may vary

Cuando hace calor, yo llevo _____ .

Cuando hace frío, yo llevo _____ .

Cuando llueve, yo llevo _____ .

4 Look at the weather symbols on the map. Then complete the sentences given below the map. The first one has been done for you.

En el norte, ___hace frío___ .   En el noreste, ___está lloviendo___ .

En el oeste, ___está nublado___ .   En el este, ___hace viento___ .

En el sur, ___hace sol___ .   En el suroeste, ___hace calor___ .

To consolidate learning, it would be useful for your child to write the date each day in Spanish and under the date, a phrase to describe the weather. By combining weather phrases with phrases to describe what they are wearing/what they are going to wear, children begin to build lengthier and more interesting sentences.

50

1 Fill in the gaps on the chart below, showing some of the subjects taught in school. **Note:** You may use a dictionary to help you.

Spanish	English
las matemáticas	maths
el teatro	drama
las ciencias	science
el español	Spanish
el dibujo	drawing
el deporte	sport

Spanish	English
la religión	R.E.
la tecnología	D.T.
la historia	history
la geografía	geography
la música	music
la informática	I.C.T.

2 Translate these English sentences into Spanish.

Sports is okay, but I hate maths.

El deporte está bien, pero odio las matemáticas.

I also like geography, because it's interesting.

También me gusta la geografía, porque es interesante.

Drawing is my favourite subject and sport is great, too!

¡El dibujo es mi asignatura favorita y también el deporte es estupendo!

I like history, but drama is awful!

Me gusta la historia, ¡pero el teatro es terrible!

51

3 Say which school subjects you like and which you dislike by filling in the gaps in these sentences. **Note:** In Spanish, any subject you mention must always have **el, la** or **las** in front of it.   Answers may vary

Me gusta _____ porque es _____ .

No me gusta _____ porque es _____ .

Me gusta mucho _____ porque es _____ .

Yo odio _____ porque es _____ .

4 Translate these Spanish expressions into English.

¡Es estupendo!   It's great!

Es interesante.   It's interesting.

Es divertido.   It's amusing.

¡Es genial!   It's great!

Es fácil.   It's easy.

Está bien.   It's okay.

Es aburrido.   It's boring.

No es bueno.   It's not good.

Es difícil.   It's difficult.

By working through these pages, children are introduced to a range of informal as well as formal phrases to express their opinion about school subjects. This will help them to use and understand Spanish as it is really spoken. These phrases can be adapted to a wide variety of situations. Encourage your child to use them to describe clothes, colours, food and hobbies.

Answers:

52–53 La música
54–55 Los números 70–1000

52

1 Add the Spanish translations of the English words to this chart, saying whether they are masculine or feminine nouns.

English	Spanish	Masculine or Feminine
clarinet	el clarinete	Masculine
saxophone	el saxofón	Masculine
piano	el piano	Masculine
guitar	la guitarra	Feminine
trumpet	la trompeta	Feminine
drums	el tambor	Masculine
violin	el violín	Masculine
cello	el violonchelo	Masculine

2 Translate these sentences into English.

Me gusta la música clásica. — I like classical music.

Me gusta mucho la música pop. — I really like pop music.

¡Me encanta la música folclórica! — I love folk music!

Me gusta también la música de ballet. — I also like ballet music.

¡No me gusta la música rock! — I don't like rock music!

53

3 Translate these sentences into Spanish. **Note:** To say that you play a musical instrument, you use the verb **tocar** (to touch) + the name of the instrument. The first one has been done for you.

I play the saxophone. — **Yo toco el saxofón.**

She plays the clarinet. — Ella toca el clarinete.

Do you play the piano? — ¿Tú tocas el piano?

He plays the violin. — Él toca el violín.

We play the trumpet. — Nosotros tocamos la trompeta.

They play the drums. — Ellos tocan el tambor.

They play the guitar. — Ellos tocan la guitarra.

4 Translate what these people are saying into English.

Yo no toco un instrumento, pero me gustan los conciertos.
I don't play an instrument, but I like concerts.

Yo no toco un instrumento, pero me encanta cantar.
I don't play an instrument, but I love singing.

Yo toco el violín en una orquesta y yo canto en un coro también.
I play the violin in an orchestra and I sing in a choir as well.

Your child needs to use the verb **tocar** to say that he or she plays a musical instrument. Compare against **jugar** or **practicar** (pages 38–39), which is used to say that one plays a sport. Remind your child to select the correct form **el** or **la** depending on whether that musical instrument is masculine or feminine.

54

1 Write the Spanish for these numbers.

70 — setenta
80 — ochenta
90 — noventa

2 Write the Spanish for these numbers.

200 — doscientos
300 — trescientos
500 — quinientos
900 — novecientos
700 — setecientos
800 — ochocientos

3 Reorder the numbers given below, starting with the smallest at the top.

veintiocho	veintiocho
sesenta y tres	treinta y dos
noventa y siete	cuarenta y uno
setenta y tres	sesenta y tres
mil	setenta y tres
ochenta y seis	ochenta y seis
treinta y dos	noventa y siete
cuarenta y uno	cien
cien	mil

55

4 Draw lines to match the numbers on the left with the number words on the right.

190 — ciento noventa
172 — ciento setenta y dos
165 — ciento sesenta y cinco
183 — ciento ochenta y tres
134 — ciento treinta y cuatro

5 Solve these sums. Give your answers first in digits and then in Spanish.

treinta y uno + cuarenta = 71 — setenta y uno
treinta + cincuenta y dos = 82 — ochenta y dos
noventa + once = 101 — ciento uno

6 Write the Spanish for each amount of money.

€ 30.80 — treinta euros con ochenta
€ 200.78 — doscientos euros con setenta y ocho
€ 86.43 — ochenta y seis euros con cuarenta y tres
€ 282.17 — doscientos ochenta y dos euros con diecisiete
€ 120.00 — ciento veinte euros

€100 €100

7 Write the year given below in Spanish.

1971 — mil novecientos setenta y uno

Make sure your child feels confident using the Spanish words for numbers up to 29 before working through these exercises. Then explain that forming larger numbers simply involves joining the tens (30, 40, 50, 60 and so on) to the ones using **y** (and). Also note that **cien** (100) becomes **ciento** before another number, such as in **ciento noventa** (190).

Answers:

56–57 La comida y las bebidas
58–59 En el café

56

① Fill in the Spanish words on the chart. Remember to put **el, la, los,** or **las** before each one. **Note:** You may use a dictionary to help you.

English	Spanish
rice	el arroz
meat	la carne
pasta	la pasta
bread	el pan
fruit	la fruta
cheese	el queso
eggs	los huevos
butter	la mantequilla
fish	el pescado
soup	la sopa
vegetables	las verduras
potatoes	las patatas
cake	la tarta
ice-cream	el helado

② Unscramble the Spanish sentences below. Then translate them into English.

queso? quieres ¿ Tú — ¿Tú quieres queso? — Do you want some cheese?

pan? ¿ Tú quieres — ¿Tú quieres pan? — Do you want some bread?

57

③ Unscramble these Spanish words to reveal a list of drinks.

al echel — la leche | le guaa — el agua
le afcé — el café | al malanodi — la limonada
el rocrefse — el refresco | el ét — el té
el etoochlac — el chocolate | le muzo de janaran — el zumo de naranja

④ Complete these sentences, using the correct Spanish translation of the English word given in brackets.

¿Vosotros tenéis arroz ? (rice) — Yo voy a tomar cereales . (cereals)

¿Vosotros tenéis aceite ? (oil) — Yo voy a tomar mermelada . (jam)

⑤ Fill in the gaps in these sentences to describe what you usually eat in a day. Answers may vary

Para mi desayuno yo como .... Yo bebo ....

Para mi almuerzo yo como .... Yo bebo ....

Para mi cena yo como .... Yo bebo ....

On these pages, your child will practise offering food at the table and asking for food items in shops. For all of these sentences, your child will need to decide if the food is masculine, feminine, singular or plural and select the right form – **el, la, los, las**. He/she can also practise using the present tense of **comer** (to eat) and **beber** (to drink) to talk about what they like or what they usually have for breakfast or lunch.

58

① Look at the Spanish words for various popular snacks and drinks in the box below. Then find them in the word-search puzzle.

bolsa de patatas | chocolate caliente | trozo de pizza
perrito caliente | bocadillo de queso | hamburguesa
helado | batido | mirinda | pan

b	z	m	k	t	r	o	z	o	d	e	p	i	z	z	a	h
o	d	a	s	d	f	g	h	j	k	l	e	w	f	r	y	b
c	v	c	u	a	b	o	q	p	h	j	r	z	o	w	m	o
a	b	h	e	l	a	d	o	i	z	v	r	x	p	d	l	l
d	n	e	k	x	t	p	e	o	f	c	i	c	a	c	p	s
i	m	t	y	s	i	k	w	u	y	r	t	v	n	v	o	a
l	d	g	h	r	d	l	y	i	q	w	o	b	m	f	i	d
l	q	m	r	a	o	l	w	k	o	r	c	r	k	r	i	e
o	e	i	a	s	f	g	h	j	k	l	a	t	g	t	y	p
d	t	r	z	c	v	x	b	n	m	l	l	y	o	g	u	a
e	y	i	c	o	g	l	a	c	e	m	i	u	r	b	j	t
q	u	n	v	i	q	r	f	o	v	b	e	i	a	n	m	a
u	i	d	d	u	a	d	h	c	a	n	o	n	y	t	t	t
e	o	e	h	z	e	o	a	u	i	t	w	g	w	r	a	
s	p	k	z	x	c	v	b	g	t	c	e	b	i	n	m	s
o	h	a	m	b	u	r	g	u	e	s	a	o	n	p	k	y
c	h	o	c	o	l	a	t	e	c	a	l	i	e	n	t	e

59

② Translate these sentences into English.

¿La carta, por favor? — Could we have the menu, please?
¿Habéis elegido? — Are you ready to order?
¿Qué queréis? — What would you like?
¿La cuenta, por favor? — Could I have the bill, please?

③ Unscramble these food orders.

una por patatas fritas, Yo favor. ración de quiero
Yo quiero una ración de patatas fritas, por favor.

queso, Yo favor. por bocadillo quiero de un
Yo quiero un bocadillo de queso, por favor.

quiero Yo de trozo un por pizza, favor.
Yo quiero un trozo de pizza, por favor.

batido, favor. un Yo por quiero
Yo quiero un batido, por favor.

④ Draw lines to match these ice-cream flavours with their English translations.

un helado de chocolate — a strawberry ice-cream
un helado de grosella — a vanilla ice-cream
un helado de fresa — a blackcurrant ice-cream
un helado de vainilla — a chocolate ice-cream

Here your child can practise ordering food and drink in a polite way. As well as speaking, it is important that children get used to understanding phrases they might hear in a shop or café. Point out to your child that when ordering ice-cream, the flavour follows the noun.

Answers:

60–61 El cuerpo
62–63 Las vacaciones
64–65 Beat the clock 3, see p.80

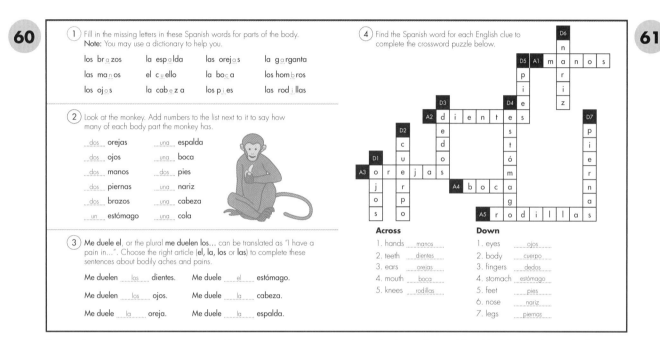

60

1 Fill in the missing letters in these Spanish words for parts of the body.
Note: You may use a dictionary to help you.

los br**a**zos	la esp**a**lda	las orej**a**s	la g**a**rganta
las ma**n**os	el c**u**ello	la bo**c**a	los hom**b**ros
los oj**o**s	la cab**e**za	los p**i**es	las rod**i**llas

2 Look at the monkey. Add numbers to the list next to it to say how many of each body part the monkey has.

dos orejas   _una_ espalda
dos ojos   _una_ boca
dos manos   _dos_ pies
dos piernas   _una_ nariz
dos brazos   _una_ cabeza
_un_ estómago   _una_ cola

3 **Me duele el**, or the plural **me duelen los…** can be translated as "I have a pain in…". Choose the right article (**el, la, los** or **las**) to complete these sentences about bodily aches and pains.

Me duelen _los_ dientes.   Me duele _el_ estómago.
Me duelen _los_ ojos.   Me duele _la_ cabeza.
Me duele _la_ oreja.   Me duele _la_ espalda.

61

4 Find the Spanish word for each English clue to complete the crossword puzzle below.

Across
1. hands — manos
2. teeth — dientes
3. ears — orejas
4. mouth — boca
5. knees — rodillas

Down
1. eyes — ojos
2. body — cuerpo
3. fingers — dedos
4. stomach — estómago
5. feet — pies
6. nose — nariz
7. legs — piernas

To say that something hurts, your child can practise using the structure **me duele/me duelen** + a body part. Remind him or her that she will need to choose the right Spanish word for "the" (**el, la, los** or **las**) depending on whether the body part is masculine, feminine, singular or plural.

62

1 Translate these sentences into Spanish.

I travelled by plane. — Yo viajé en avión.
He travelled by car. — Él viajó en coche.
We travelled by boat. — Nosotros viajamos en barco.

2 Translate these sentences into Spanish.

Pierre went to Italy. — Pedro fue a Italia.
Sophie went to France. — Sofía fue a Francia.
My sisters went to Africa. — Mis hermanas fueron a África.
My parents went to Portugal. — Mis padres fueron a Portugal.

3 Choose the correct form of the perfect tense of **ir** (to go) to complete these sentences.

Nosotros _fuimos_ a una iglesia.
Él _fue_ a un castillo.
Ellas _fueron_ a la playa.
Vosotros _fuisteis_ al museo.
Yo _fui_ a un lago.

63

4 Here are some useful Spanish expressions to help you say what you thought about some of the things you did on holiday. Draw lines to match them to their English translations.

Fue divertido. — It was funny.
Fue pesado. — It was dull.
Fue rápido. — It was fast.
¡Fue apasionante! — It was exciting!
Fue terrorífico. — It was frightening.
¡Fue genial! — It was great!

5 You may have visited an amusement park while on holiday. Choose the correct form of the perfect tense of **ver** (to see) to complete these sentences and say what your family saw on the ghost-train ride. Then write the English translation.

Mi hermana _vio_ un hombre lobo.
My sister saw a werewolf.

Mi hermano _vio_ un vampiro.
My brother saw a vampire.

Mis padres _vieron_ unas arañas.
My parents saw some spiders.

Yo _vi_ un esqueleto.
I saw a skeleton.

Explain to your child that as in the present tense, there are different endings for the past tense depending on the subject of the sentence. It might be useful to run through the different forms of the past tense of the verbs used on these pages, especially those that are irregular, such as **ir** (to go).

Answers:

20–21 Beat the clock 1
42–43 Beat the clock 2
64–65 Beat the clock 3

20 / 21

Verb	Answer	Verb	Answer	Verb	Answer	Verb	Answer
Yo (comer)	como	Él (comer)	come	Ella (meter)	mete	Ellas (comprender)	comprenden
Ella (prometer)	promete	Yo (romper)	rompo	Vosotros (comer)	coméis	Ella (responder)	responde
Tú (romper)	rompes	Nosotros (romper)	rompemos	Yo (responder)	respondo	Ellos (aprender)	aprenden
Él (comprender)	comprende	Él (romper)	rompe	Tú (responder)	respondes	Vosotros (prometer)	prometéis
Él (prometer)	promete	Tú (prometer)	prometes	Él (vender)	vende	Nosotros (aprender)	aprendemos
Tú (comer)	comes	Ella (aprender)	aprende	Él (meter)	mete	Vosotros (comprender)	comprendéis
Nosotros (comer)	comemos	Ellos (comer)	comen	Tú (meter)	metes	Vosotros (apender)	aprendéis
Vosotros (correr)	corréis	Ella (comer)	come	Tú (depender)	dependes	Nosotros (meter)	metemos
Ellos (romper)	rompen	Él (aprender)	aprende	Ella (romper)	rompe	Nosotros (comprender)	comprendemos
Ellos (prometer)	prometen	Vosotros (romper)	rompéis	Tú (vender)	vendes	Ellos (comprender)	comprenden
Ellas (romper)	rompen	Él (responder)	responde	Ellas (prometer)	prometen	Ella (comprender)	comprende
Él (correr)	corre	Ellas (aprender)	aprenden	Ellas (comer)	comen	Vosotros (depender)	dependéis
Yo (correr)	corro	Yo (vender)	vendo	Él (depender)	depende	Nosotros (prometer)	prometemos
Tú (aprender)	aprendes	Tú (comprender)	comprendes	Yo (meter)	meto	Nosotros (depender)	dependemos

42 / 43

Verb	Answer	Verb	Answer	Verb	Answer	Verb	Answer
Yo (vivir)	vivo	Ella (insistir)	insiste	Él (vivir)	vive	Yo (permitir)	permito
Tú (existir)	existes	Él (permitir)	permite	Nosotros (existir)	existimos	Él (existir)	existe
Él (insistir)	insiste	Tú (vivir)	vives	Tú (insistir)	insistes	Ella (decidir)	decide
Nosotros (vivir)	vivimos	Yo (existir)	existo	Vosotros (permitir)	permitís	Ella (vivir)	vive
Ellos (existir)	existen	Ellos (insistir)	insisten	Él (decidir)	decide	Vosotros (insistir)	insistís
Ella (permitir)	permite	Ellos (permitir)	permiten	Él (subir)	sube	Ellas (decidir)	deciden
Yo (decidir)	decido	Tú (decidir)	decides	Ella (sufrir)	sufre	Tú (permitir)	permites
Nosotros (decidir)	decidimos	Vosotros (vivir)	vivís	Ellas (vivir)	viven	Ellos (vivir)	viven
Yo (subir)	subo	Tú (subir)	subes	Nosotros (permitir)	permiten	Vosotros (existir)	existís
Él (compartir)	comparte	Él (sufrir)	sufre	Tú (compartir)	compartes	Ella (subir)	sube
Tú (sufrir)	sufres	Tú (recibir)	recibes	Él (recibir)	recibe	Nosotros (sufrir)	sufrimos
Ella (existir)	existe	Yo (compartir)	comparto	Ellos (decidir)	deciden	Él (compartir)	comparte
Nosotros (recibir)	recibimos	Vosotros (decidir)	decidís	Ellos (existir)	existen	Vosotros (recibir)	recibís
Ellas (permitir)	permiten	Yo (insistir)	insisto	Nosotros (insistir)	insistimos	Ellas (insistir)	insisten

64 / 65

Verb	Answer	Verb	Answer	Verb	Answer	Verb	Answer
Yo (hablar)	hablo	Ella (quedar)	queda	Él (hablar)	habla	Yo (llamar)	llamo
Tú (pasar)	pasas	Él (llamar)	llama	Nosotros (pasar)	pasamos	Él (pasar)	pasa
Él (quedar)	queda	Tú (hablar)	hablas	Tú (quedar)	quedar	Ella (mirar)	mira
Nosotros (hablar)	hablamos	Yo (pasar)	paso	Vosotros (llamar)	llamáis	Ella (hablar)	habla
Ellos (pasar)	pasan	Ellos (quedar)	quedan	Él (mirar)	mira	Vosotros (quedar)	quedáis
Ella (llamar)	llama	Ellos (llamar)	llaman	Él (entrar)	entra	Ellas (mirar)	miran
Yo (mirar)	miro	Tú (mirar)	miras	Ella (tomar)	toma	Tú (llamar)	llamas
Nosotros (mirar)	miramos	Vosotros (hablar)	habláis	Ellas (hablar)	hablan	Ellos (hablar)	hablan
Yo (entrar)	entro	Tú (entrar)	entras	Nosotros (llamar)	llamamos	Vosotros (pasar)	pasáis
Él (trabajar)	trabaja	Él (tomar)	toma	Tú (trabajar)	trabajas	Ella (entrar)	entra
Tú (tomar)	tomas	Tú (comprar)	compras	Él comprar	compra	Nosotros (tomar)	tomamos
Ella (pasar)	pasa	Yo (trabajar)	trabajo	Ellos (mirar)	miran	Él (trabajar)	trabaja
Nosotros (comprar)	compramos	Vosotros (mirar)	miráis	Ellas (pasar)	pasan	Vosotros (comprar)	compráis
Ellas (llamar)	llaman	Yo (quedar)	quedo	Nosotros (quedar)	quedamos	Ellas (quedar)	quedan

These "Beat the clock" pages test your child's ability to quickly recall the lessons learned. The tests require your child to work under some pressure. As with most tests of this type, tell your child before he or she starts not to get stuck on one question, but to move on and return to the tricky one later if time allows. Encourage your child to record his or her score and the time taken to complete the test. You can also encourage your child to retake the test later to see if he or she can improve on his or her previous attempt.